AF348616

DARJA BAJAGIĆ

It Takes an Island
to Feel This Good

Potrebno je ostrvo
za ovako dobar osjećaj

Pavilion of Montenegro
60th International Art Exhibition –
La Biennale di Venezia
20.04 - 24.11.2024.

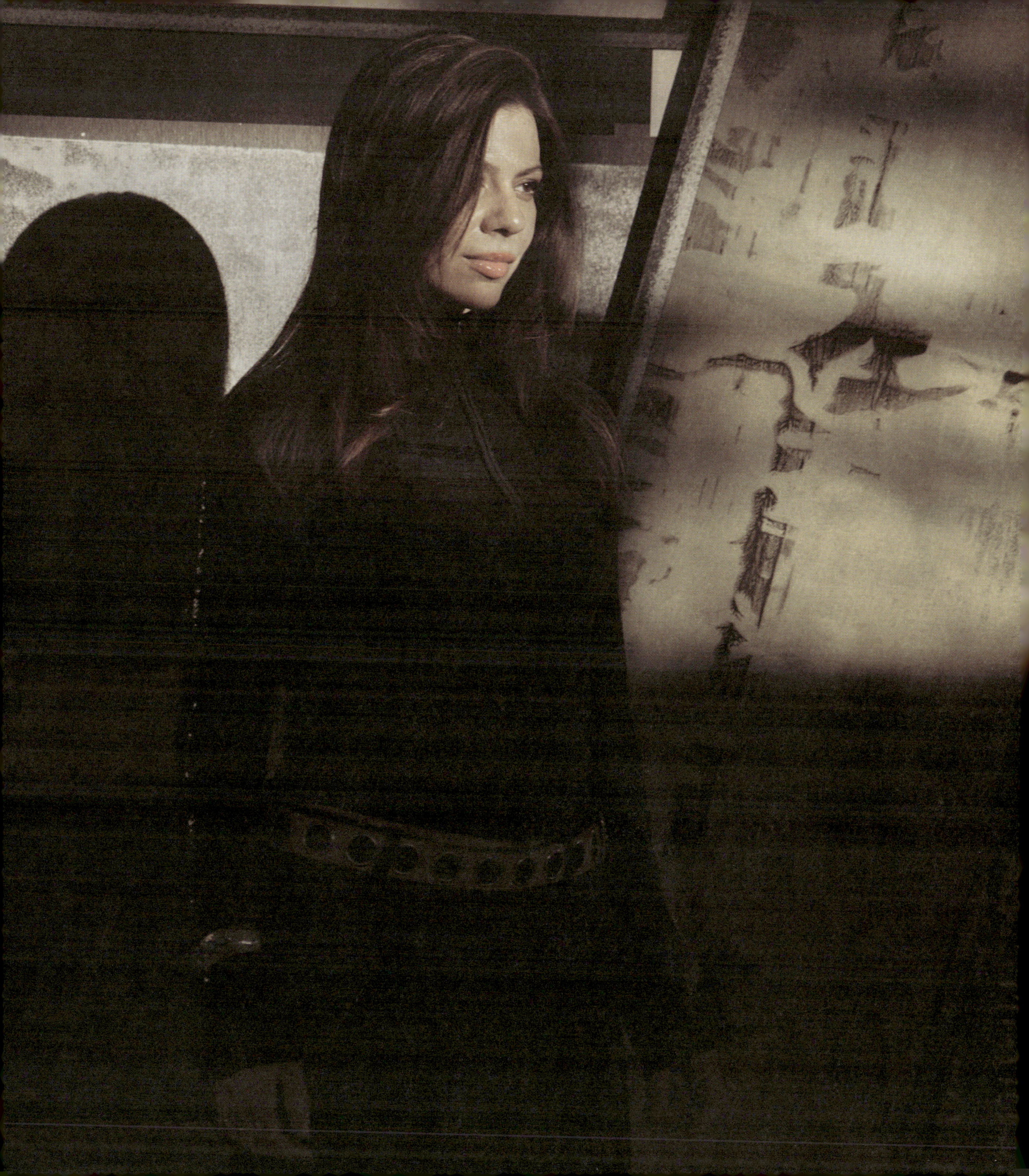

Mamula, a military fortress built in the 19th century, is named after Austro-Hungarian general Lazar Mamula, who supervised its construction.

Anchored in the Adriatic Sea, between the Montenegrin peninsulas of Prevlaka and Luštica, Mamula fortress served as a key component of the Austro-Hungarian army's strategies to protect the Bay of Kotor from potential enemy breakthroughs.

The circular-shaped fortress covers ninety percent of the island's total area, measuring 200 meters in diameter.

During the turbulent times of the First World War, Mamula served as a prison, and this function was partially retained during the Second World War when the fascist regime of the Kingdom of Italy under Benito Mussolini repurposed it into a concentration camp.

In 2023, Mamula was reopened as a luxury hotel.

Mamula, vojna tvrđava izgrađena je u 19. vijeku, nosi ime po austrougarskom generalu Lazaru Mamuli koji je nadgledao njenu izgradnju.

Usidrena u Jadranskom moru, između crnogorskih poluostrva Prevlaka i Luštica, tvrđava Mamula služila je kao ključna komponenta strategije austougarske vojske za zaštitu Boke Kotorske od potencijalnih proboja neprijatelja.

Tvrđava kružnog oblika pokriva devedeset odsto površine ostrva koja iznosi ukupno 200m u prečniku.

Tokom turbulentnih vremena Prvog svjetskog rata, Mamula je služila kao zatvor, a ta funkcija djelimično je zadržana tokom Drugog svjetskog rata, kada ju je fašistički režim Kraljevine Italije Benita Musolinija prekrojio u koncentracioni logor.

Godine 2023. Mamula je otvorena kao luksuzni hotel.

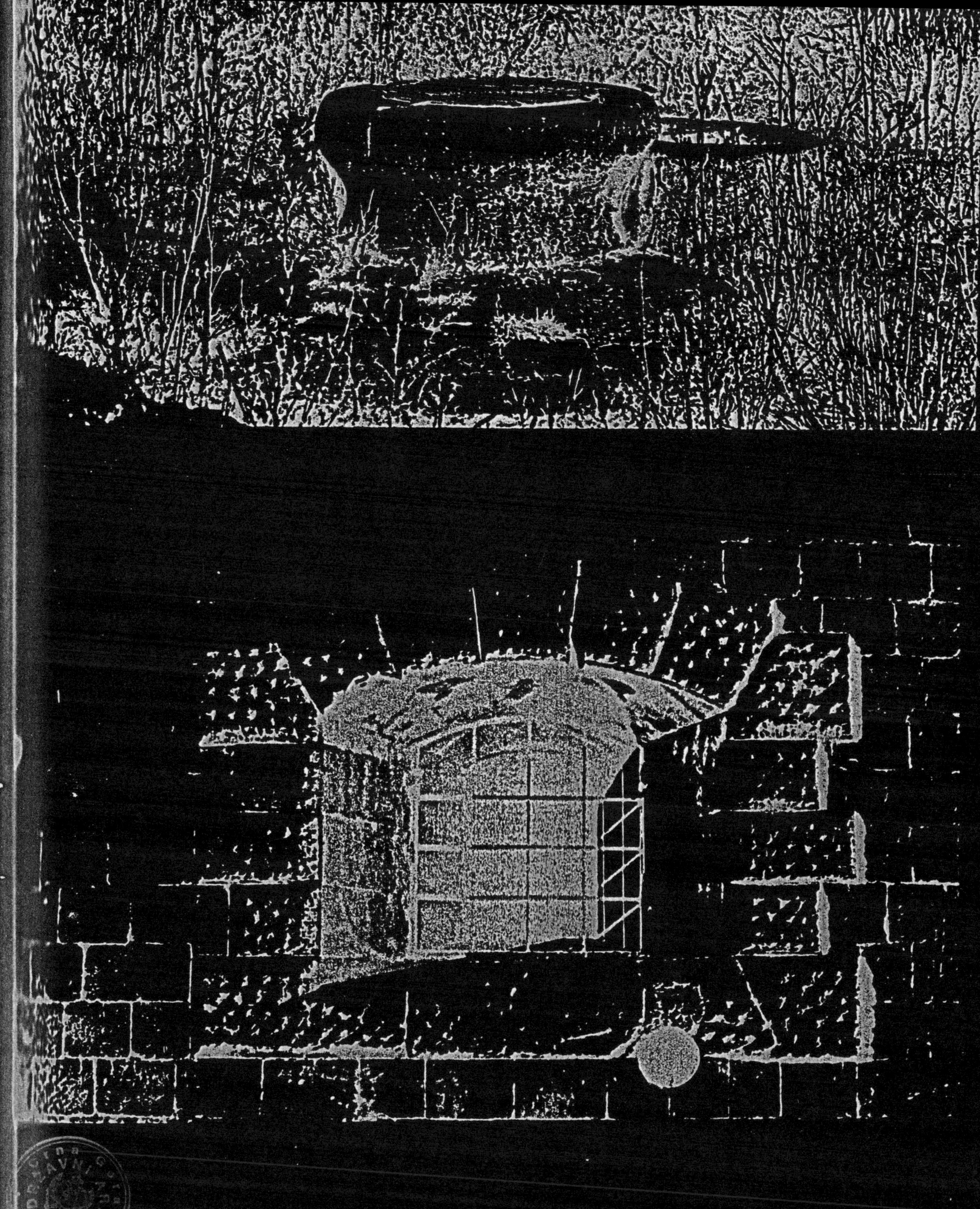

CONTENTS
SADRŽAJ

FORWARD

Lastavica or Velika Žanjica is a circular island situated at the mouth of the Bay of Kotor. It spans a mere 200 meters in diameter, with a fortress occupying ninety percent of its surface area. The fortress boasts a centuries-old history, having undergone several transformations over time. Originally erected in 1853 as a fortification to safeguard the territories of Austria-Hungary, it was commissioned by general Lazar Mamula, after whom both the fortress and the island were named. Subsequently, it served as a prison during World War I and functioned as a concentration camp during the fascist occupation from 1942 to 1943. In 2015, following decades of neglect, the Montenegrin parliament awarded a 49-year concession to a Swiss-Egyptian company, which subsequently converted it into a luxury hotel.

An inscription placed at the entrance to the fortress in 1965 remains there to this day, reading:

> "Neither darkness nor mold, neither hunger nor torture, neither the infamous occupier's courts nor executions have broken the faith in the victory of those imprisoned here during the two World Wars. Over one thousand and five hundred fighters and participants of the People's Liberation Struggle from all parts of our country, from 1941 to 1943, endured the most terrible hardships in the prison cells of this fortress, proving how to fight and die for the bright future of our peoples—for socialism. Their conduct before the enemy on this proud and sorrowful island will serve as an example of struggle and sacrifice for the freedom and welfare of their homeland. The people of the Bay of Kotor."

Ana Simona Zelenović

UVOD

Lastavica ili Velika Žanjica, je kružno ostvo smješteno na samom ulazu u Boku Kotorsku, prečnika svega 200 m sa tvrđavom koja zauzima devedeset posto njegove površine. Tvrđava ima viševjekovnu istoriju tokom koje joj je namjena bila nekoliko puta mijenjana - kao utvrđenje za odbranu Austrougarske osnovao ju je 1853. general Lazar Mamula, po kome tvrđava i ostrvo dobijaju kasniji naziv, te je potom služila kao zatvor tokom Prvog svjetskog rata, a kao koncentracioni logor za vrijeme fašističke okupacije 1942-43, da bi nakon decenija zapuštenosti, odlukom crnogorskog Parlamenta 2015. bila data na koncesiju na 49 godina švajcarsko-egipatskoj kompaniji koja je od nje načinila luksuzni hotel.

Na samom ulazu u tvrđavu i danas stoji natpis postavljen 1965. godine:
> "Ni mrak ni memla, ni glad ni mučenja, ni zloglasni okupatorski sudovi ni strijeljanja nisu slomili vjeru u pobjedu onih koji su ovdje tamnovali u dva svjetska rata. Preko hiljadu i pet stotina boraca i učesnika narodnooslobodilačke borbe iz svih krajeva naše zemlje u periodu od 1941. do 1943. doživjeli su u zatvorskim ćelijama ove tvrđave najstrašnije muke dokazujući kako se bori i mre za sreću budućnost naših naroda – za socijalizam. Njihovo držanje pred neprijateljem na ovom ponosnom i tužnom ostrvu služiće kao primjer borbe i žrtvovanja za slobodu i dobro svoje domovine. Narod Boke kotorske."

Ana Simona Zelenović

IT TAKES A PAINTING TO FEEL THIS BAD

Ana Simona Zelenović

Indeed, the past would fully befall only a resurrected humanity. Said another way: only for a resurrected humanity would its past, in each of its moments, be citable. Each of its lived moments becomes a citation a l'ordre du jour [order of the day]—whose day is precisely that of the Last Judgment.

— Walter Benjamin

It Takes an Island to Feel This Good is an exhibition featuring five paintings and one sculpture by Darja Bajagić. Born in Podgorica, Montenegro, she was raised in Cairo, Egypt, and received her formal education in the United States. Today, she lives and works in Montenegro. Her relationship with her heterogeneous heritage is twofold. She exists on both sides of heritage: as someone who imprints it into her work, thereby revising, preserving, and transmitting it, and, on the other hand, as someone who never fully belongs to any one culture, an eternal stranger, an observer without participation. This dual position prompts the artist to approach each series of works as a researcher, aiming to understand a phenomenon from all angles before offering her interpretation. This approach extends to the current topic at hand. The paintings, stemming from the artist's two-year investigation of the island of Mamula in the State Archives of Montenegro and the analysis of media coverage regarding its contemporary repurposing, delve into the history of heritage and contemporary attitudes toward it. The series' title is derived from an advertisement for the new luxury hotel, ironically referencing the layers of history of the fortress, which transformed from a prison and a concentration camp into a resort. Through themes of collective memory, history, and the present, Darja Bajagić's thoughtful approach presents us with a reflection of ourselves, highlighting all the potential, and particularly undesirable, implications of that reflection.

***

The specific manner in which Bajagić constructs a painting originates from her approach to phenomena. The relationship between research and subject matter transitions from content analysis to the layering of form. Duality and ambiguity have characterized her method since the inception of her career, and the impossibility of fully grasping the meaning and the position of the artist is integral to her artistic message, which shapes the visual expression of her works. *The Ambivalence of the Sacred* (2024) is a paradigmatic example of how a narrative without protagonists continues to cultivate an atmosphere on a formal level, offering an introduction to how visual elements are handled in other works. Despite its self-referential nature, the works' visual attributes—shapes, dark hues, and particularly subtle variations in shades—evoke a desire to come nearer, to contemplate further, and to delve into the hidden meanings that unveil themselves upon prolonged observation from various perspectives. The layered nature of the works further complicates the understanding of their meaning: in addition to the purely formal, the artist adds two more iconographic layers, offering only hints for interpretation. Regarding the paintings *Frustum — Numero 11: Komadat Logora Mamula (Piece of Mamula Camp)* or *Komandat Logora Mamula (Commander of Mamula Camp)* (2024), *Gateway to the Gulf* (2024), *The Murder of the Sign* (2024), and *Threshold (Gigantomachy Concerning a Void)* (2024), we know that they contain xeroxes from the State Archives of Montenegro. In the exhibition, we lack precise information about who, exactly, is depicted; we only have information about their visible roles: commander, prisoners, and the fortress itself, which we know had changing functions—a fact that the third layer, the iconological layer of meaning, entirely leaves to the interpretation of the observer. Anchored in the first, formal layer, and the second, iconographic one, we examine the depictions: number 11, known as the serial number under which Mamula camp was registered in the fascist administration, becomes a framework for observing its commander; two photographs of the island depicting the fortress are amalgamated by a line, simultaneously dividing and uniting them, emblematic of marking presence and absence in the documentation of prisoners; the photographs of the prisoners are framed by the shapes of the works themselves—one by an exclamation mark, the other by a rectangle. We interpret all the representations in congruence with the works' formal properties; the textures and shapes of the canvases and frames, serving as the material layer, are integrated into the meaning. Raw canvases, which do not have an originally painterly purpose but rather a practical, sometimes even military one, together with the steel structures that frame them, point to the brutalistic aesthetics of the raw material itself; instead of embellishment, we witness the need to incorporate the associativity of the material into the meaning of the work. The shape of the painting becomes a sign, even a symbol—it directs towards the key in which the representation is interpreted, determining the angle of observation. The photographs, scanned and enlarged, but in their original state, are placed in a dialogue with visual interventions: materials, signs, shapes, compositional juxtapositions, imposed frames, and finally, in one part of the painting, the artist's painterly interventions.

In the presence of the works, already at first contact, the atmosphere swiftly engulfs the exhibition space, permeating the gaps between the paintings and the viewer's perception. The colors of the canvases, combinations of blues, grays, reds, and rust hues, convey the gravity of the subject matter. The grainy textures of enlarged printed photographs occasionally resemble abstract compositions; in *Gateway to the Gulf* (2024), the forms are blended to the point of unrecognizability. This sense of uncertainty breeds tension. Upon initial observation, we catch glimpses of the themes within the works: clear associations arise from the bullet holes in the steel frame of *Gateway to the Gulf* (2024); the sculpture *Limb Immobilizer (Iron Rings to Which Some Prisoners Were Tied)* (2024) replicating shackles from the fortress's facade; and the "point" of the painting *Threshold (Gigantomachy Concerning a Void)* (2024)—the painting shaped like an exclamation mark—whose abstract blend of materials resembles an open wound. Thus, even without prior knowledge, the obscure atmosphere simultaneously encourages further research into the works' meaning, albeit tinged with a sense of fear and quiet unease.

The dominant theme—the relationship to historical heritage and collective memory—also aligns with other important subjects: the relationship to Evil, and questions of human and political responsibility towards others and memory. Walter Benjamin observes: "To articulate what is past does not mean to recognize 'how it really was.' It means to take control of a memory, as it flashes in a moment of danger."[1] Darja Bajagić does not

1   Walter Benjamin, *Illuminations* (New York: Schocken Books, 1969).

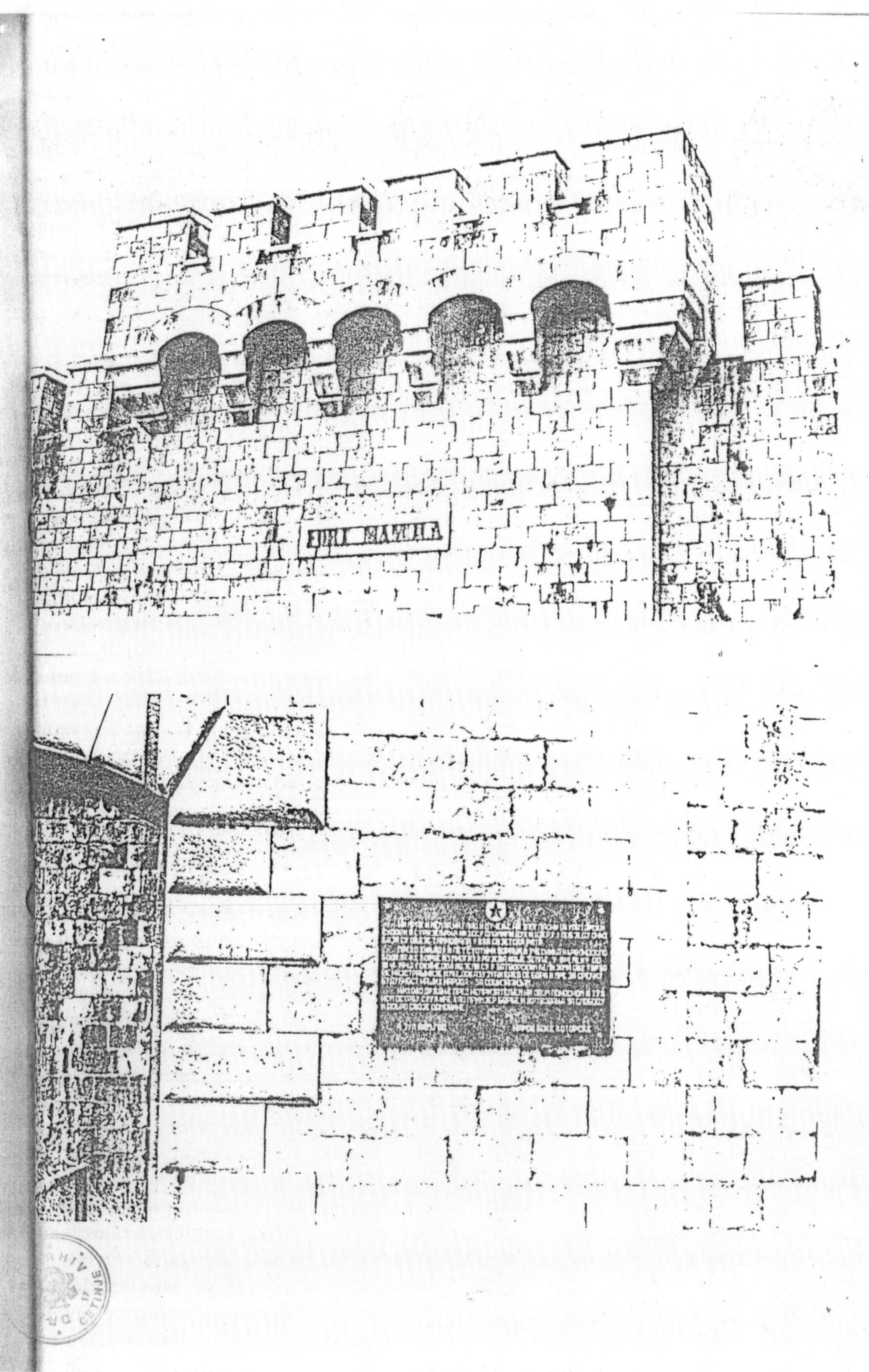

Scan of a photocopy of a document
with an undated photograph of Mamula
island from the State Archives of Montenegro (research material of the artist).

Sken fotokopije dokumenta sa nedatiranom fotografijom ostrva Mamula iz
Državnog arhiva Crne Gore (istraživački
materijal umjetnice).

presume to use the archival material to address the notion of testimony; she simply evokes this moment of danger as always possible. The paintings before us are not memories; they are artistic visions that, using historical evidence, remind us of what we think we have avoided. Susan Sontag says that there is no such thing as collective memory, but only individual memory and collective instruction.[2] How historical events, like the suffering in fascist and Nazi camps, are remembered and interpreted in public discourse is heavily influenced by political and ideological power dynamics. But regardless of the crime being remembered or forgotten, the principle is the same—"these villains are not us." History unfolds within the vacuum of specific circumstances and individuals. As observers from a significant distance, we might consider ourselves innocent witnesses to its unfolding. Yet Bajagić's paintings from this series subvert this attitude. Evil(doing) happens always and everywhere.

"The camp is the space that is opened when the state of exception begins to become the rule," concludes Giorgio Agamben, it's a space where the law is completely suspended.[3] The camp is the inscribing of the naked life itself into the order—"a sign of the system's inability to function without being transformed into a lethal machine."[4] His definitions imply that the camp is embedded within order itself, functioning as a concealed matrix of politics in which we still live. It is this structure of the camp that we must learn to recognize in all its metamorphoses.[5] In his book *The Transparency of Evil*, Baudrillard argues that in a society where it is impossible to talk about Evil, Evil has metamorphosed into a viral and terrorist form that haunts us. He poses the question: *Where did Evil go?*— and answers: *Everywhere*.[6] Both Agamben and Baudrillard depart from the naïve image of the world, politics, and society, where there are "victims" and "aggressors," where a polarized view of reality divides us all into "innocent" and "guilty," warning of the seductiveness of Evil (Enemy) and the danger of approaching from a distance, from the point of moral correctness. While Agamben warns that, sooner or later, we will start to identify with an enemy whose structure we don't know, Baudrillard says that Evil must be fought the same way—with Evil. If we lose our connection with Evil, if we stop identifying with it, there are two possibilities for us—to die, with no immunity, at the slightest contact with the world, or to start unconsciously reproducing it.

Bajagić invites us to reconsider the hypocrisy in turning away from Evil and evil-doing, whether contemporary or historical. The subject's unclear position in dealing with what happened (since it was allowed to happen) calls for responsibility. There are no innocent bystanders. Initially, the paintings evoke a sense of chill and fear, which then give way to feelings of anger, pain, and shame. If we have still managed to maintain ourselves as moral observers, the anger is directed towards the historical enemy— fascism, and its modern equivalent—oblivion. Out of anger and suffering, we pose the question: *How were such barbarities committed in the 20th century? Or: How can a man commit such crimes against another?* The two aforementioned philosophers highlight the hypocrisy and naiveté of such inquiries. Agamben suggests that the question we should pose is, in fact, "which legal procedures and dispositifs of power made this possible," while Baudrillard emphasizes that "barbarities" are not merely irrational episodes of humanity but rather align with [the] social aspirations of plunging into the abyss. If we abandon hypocrisy, three options remain: suffering, shame, or fear. Shame compels us to acknowledge and confront, to accept responsibility, regardless of our inclination. Fear, on the other hand, prompts us to close our eyes to horrors and creates distance between ourselves and others. The observer can always adapt as well. We are accustomed to shielding ourselves from the unsettling, closing our eyes to the dreadful realities we know are occurring. However, humans also possess a need to grieve, as the narrative of pathos is deeply ingrained in discourse and carries a healing

2   Susan Sontag, *Regarding the Pain of Others* (Harlow: Penguin Books, 2004), 74.

3   The important thing that Agamben points out in the emergence of camps (both in the *campos concetracio-nes* that the Spaniards created in Cuba in 1896 and concentration camps into which the Englishmen put the Boers at the beginning of the 20th century) is that they emerge from the state of exception, its expansion to the whole civil society. (Agamben, 2020)

4   Giorgio Agamben, *Homo Sacer: Sovereign Power and Bare Life*, trans. Daniel Heller-Roazen (Stanford: Stanford University Press,1998).

5   Giorgio Agamben, *State of Exception* (Chicago: University of Chicago Press, 2005).

6   Jean Baudrillard, *Transparency of Evil* (London:Verso, 1993), 81.

influence. Discussing the portrayal of horror and pathos in depictions of suffering, Sontag writes, "So far as we feel sympathy, we feel we are not accomplices to what caused the suffering."[7] "Those with a stomach to look are playing a role authorized by many glorious depictions of suffering. Torment, a canonical subject in art, is often represented as a spectacle, something being watched (or ignored) by other people. The implication is: no, it cannot be stopped."[8] It is a grim reality, an intrinsic part of life, but it is not happening to me. This marks the limit of our responsibility, as well as the absence of fear—the suffering endured by others is physically and historically distant, presenting no immediate threat. After we have finished lamenting over the world's horrors, we can resume our virtuous lives, absolved by our suffering on behalf of others. *It's not happening to me because I don't deserve it, I am good.*

Facing the dreadful is different. It does not offer healing. Instead, it forces a choice between bystander passivity or cowardice, closing our eyes to avoid witnessing the scene. The work of Darja Bajagić has always featured the iconography of suffering, intertwined with picturesque horror. Hence, her paintings resemble a minefield. Without understanding their implications, they deter impulsive reactions and demand strategic thinking, self-awareness, and reflection. The boundaries between us and the depicted, between reality and fiction, between history and the present, remain unclear, thus invoking fear that Evil is encroaching upon reality, that it envelops us, perhaps even resides within us, yet unrecognized. Uncertainty and ignorance give form to the Devil. *What if I am Evil?*

The ambiguity evoked by the paintings regarding the observer's position generates the anxiety that is the Hell of our time. We lack sufficient information to ascertain whether we stand on the right side, and if, by chance, we find ourselves inadvertently aligned with the wrong side, we are unable to choose. We lack the means to determine our error, lack the strength to shoulder blame, and lack the courage to assume responsibility. We possess no pre-established evidence of our innocence, nor the opportunity to resolve the dilemma. Consequently, we remain ontologically paralyzed, incapable of assuming any of the roles presented—victims, aggressors, observers (accomplices), or innocent bystanders.

One might assume that a subject as stark as the transformation of a former concentration camp into a luxury hotel offers little room for nuanced exploration. However, for Bajagić, this gray area is precisely the focus of her artistic endeavor. Her approach is a transgressive one, which many artists shy away from due to contemporary society's increasingly polarized view of reality. This view often dictates a singular "right side of history," with moral correctness that remains unchallenged. By creating works that challenge both the observer and their perceptions of the phenomenon, Bajagić restores art's role in prompting engagement. Through art, she elevates collective memory and personal historical connections to a meta-level. Here, the precise time and place of Evil become less significant, replaced instead by a reflection on our involvement and the emotions it evokes. This new epistemology is not solely intellectual; it is visceral and emotional. Art interrupts judgment, urging introspection and a reevaluation of one's stance. It beckons for involvement, prompting moments of reflection and silence. Bajagić adeptly reminds us of history's intricacies and nuances, our role in its contemporary context, and the absence of moral innocence. By recognizing Evil within ourselves, viewing it as a continuum rather than a distant "other," and appreciating its seductiveness, we open the door to its prevention. In doing so, we can "deliver tradition anew from the conformism which is on the point of overwhelming it."[9]

7   Sontag , ibid. p 36.

8   Sontag, ibid. p 36.

9   Benjamin, ibid.

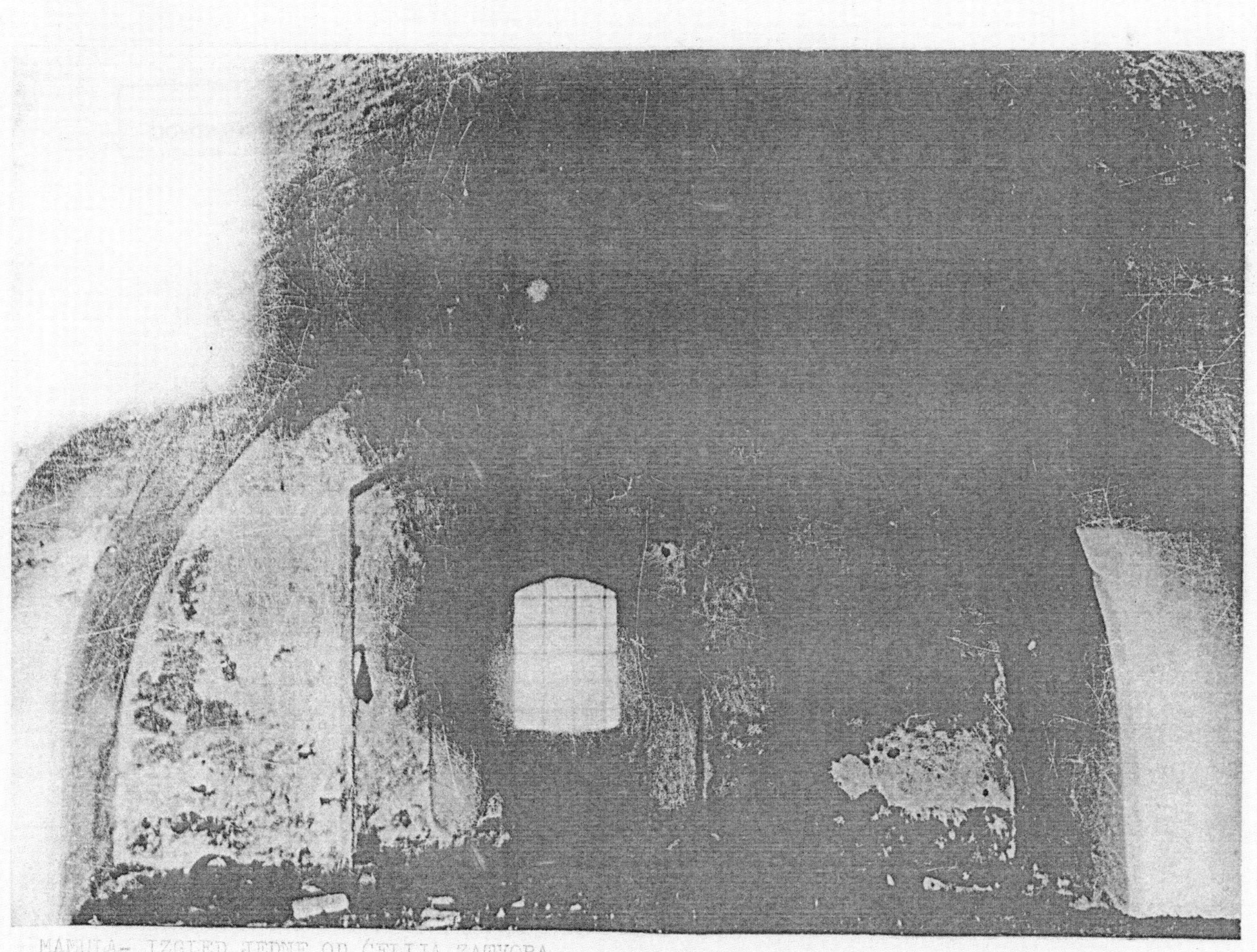

Scan of a photocopy of a document with an undated photograph of Mamula island from the State Archives of Montenegro (research material of the artist). The original image caption reads, "Mamula- Appearance of one of the prison cells."

Sken fotokopije dokumenta sa nedatiranom fotografijom ostrva Mamula iz Državnog arhiva Crne Gore (istraživački materijal umjetnice). Originalni opis slike glasi: "Mamula - Izgled jedne od ćelija zatvora".

BIBLIOGRAPHY:

Agamben, Giorgio. *Šta je logor?* 2020. Beograd: Fakultet za medije i komunikacije.
Agamben, Giorgio. *State of Exception.* Chicago: University of Chicago Press, 2005.Agamben, Giorgio. *Homo Sacer: Sovereign Power and Bare Life.* Translated by Daniel Heller-Roazen. Stanford: Stanford University Press, 1998.
Agamben, Giorgio. *Remnants of Auschwitz: The Witness and the Archive.* Translated by Daniel Heller-Roazen. New York: Zone Books, 1999.
Benjamin, Walter, *Illuminations.* New York: Schocken Books, 1969.
Baudrillard, Jean. The Transparency of Evil. London: Verso, 1993.
Sontag, Susan. Regarding the Pain of Others. Harlow: Penguin Books, 2004.

Mamula.
Forts am Scoglio Rondoni im Einfahrtskanal der Bocche di Cattaro. Fig 2
Blatt
Nro 3
Rectificiert für das Jahr
Cattaro im December 1890
K. UND K. GENIEDIRECTION
IN CATTARO
Grundriss
Dalmatien

"The camp is the space that is opened when the state of exception begins to become the rule," concludes Giorgio Agamben, it's a space where the law is completely suspended. The camp is the inscribing of the naked life itself into the order—"a sign of the system's inability to function without being transformed into a lethal machine." His definitions imply that the camp is embedded within order itself, functioning as a concealed matrix of politics in which we still live. It is this structure of the camp that we must learn to recognize in all its metamorphoses.

„Logor je prostor koji se otvara kada stanje izuzeća počinje da postaje pravilo", zaključuje Đorđo Agamben; to je prostor gdje je zakon u cjelosti suspendovan. Logor je upisivanje samog golog života u poredak – „znak nemogućnosti sistema da funkcioniše a da se ne transformiše u smrtonosnu mašinu". Implikacija njegovih definicija jeste da je logor utisnut u sâm poredak kao skrivena matrica politike u kojoj i dalje živimo i koju moramo naučiti da prepoznajemo u svim njenim metamorfozama.

POTREBNA JE SLIKA ZA OVAKO LOŠ OSJEĆAJ

Ana Simona Zelenović

> *Tek iskupljenom čovečanstvu potpuno pripada njegova prošlost.*
> *To znači: tek iskupljeno čovečanstvo može citirati svoju prošlost u svakom trenutku.*
> *Svaki njegov proživljeni trenutak postaje* citation a l′ordre du jour
> *— a taj dan je upravo dan poslednjeg suda.*
>
> **— Valter Benjamin**

It Takes an Island to Feel This Good je izložba pet slika i jedne skulpture Darje Bajagić, umjetnice porijeklom iz Podgorice, odrasle u Egiptu a školovane u SAD, koja sada ponovo živi i radi u Crnoj Gori. Njen odnos prema sopstvenom heterogenom nasljeđu je dvojak – ona je uvijek sa obje strane nasljeđa – neko ko ga utiskuje u rad (čime ga preispituje, čuva i prenosi) i, sa druge strane, neko ko nikada do kraja ne pripada jednoj kulturi – vječiti stranac, posmatrač bez učestvovanja. Dvostruka pozicija autorku nagoni da svakoj seriji radova pristupa istraživački, da sagledava fenomen sa svih strana prije nego što ponudi sopstvenu interpretaciju. Tako je i sa temom koja je pred nama – o istoriji baštine i savremenom odnosu prema njoj govori ciklus slika nastao nakon autorkinog dvogodišnjeg istraživanja ostrva Mamula u crnogorskim arhivima i analize medijskog izvještavanja o njegovoj savremenoj prenamjeni. Sâm naslov serije preuzet je iz reklame za novi luksuzni hotel, a ironično govori o odnosu prema slojevima istorije tvrđave koja je od zatvora i logora postala odmaralište. Darja Bajagić u svom promišljenom maniru predstavlja teme kao što su odnos prema kolektivnom sjećanju, istoriji i današnjici, slika nas samih sa svim mogućim, a prije svega nepoželjnim implikacijama tog odraza.

***

Specifičnost načina na koji Bajagić gradi sliku proizilazi iz njenog pristupa fenomenima. Istraživački odnos prema materiji kreće se iz analize sadržaja do slojevitosti forme. Dvostrukost i ambiguitet odlikuju njen postupak od samih početaka karijere; nemogućnost da se ikad do kraja iščitaju značenje i pozicija umjetnice za nju su dio umjetničke poruke, što doprinosi i samoj likovnosti radova. *The Ambivalence of the Sacred* (2024) paradigmatičan je primer načina na koji predstava bez aktera i dalje radi na stvaranju atmosfere na nivou formalnog i svojevrsni je uvod u način na koji su likovni elementi tretirani u ostalim radovima. Iako je samoreferentna, ona proizvodi svojim likovnim kvalitetima – oblikom, tamnim bojama i ponajviše jedva uočljivim razlikama u nijansama – težnju da joj se priđe bliže, da se o njoj više promisli, da se pronikne u skriveno značenje koje će se otkriti ako u nju gledamo dovoljno dugo i iz svih uglova. Slojevitost radova komplikuje i razumijevanje značenja: pored čisto formalnog, autorka dodaje još dva ikonografska sloja nudeći samo naznake za tumačenje. Ono što znamo o slikama *Frustum — Numero 11: Komadat Logora Mamula (Piece of Mamula*

Camp) or Komandat Logora Mamula (Commander of Mamula Camp) (2024), Gateway to the Gulf (2024), The Murder of the Sign (2024), Threshold (Gigantomachy Concerning a Void) (2024) jeste da su na njima xeroxi iz crnogorskih arhiva. Na izložbi nemamo precizne podatke o tome ko je tačno prikazan, imamo samo informacije o njihovim vidljivim funkcijama: komandant, zatvorenici i sâm objekat tvrđave, za koju znamo da je mijenjala funkcije – što treći sloj, ikonološki sloj značenja, ostavlja u potpunosti tumačenju posmatrača. Oslonjeni na prvi, formalni sloj, i drugi, ikonografski, posmatramo prikaze: broj 11, za koji znamo da je redni broj pod kojim je logor Mamula zaveden u fašističkoj administraciji, postaje okvir za posmatranje njegovog Komandanta; dvije fotografije ostrva sa tvrđavom spojene su u jedinstvenu cjelinu crtom, koja ih ujedno i razdvaja i spaja, a koja je karakterističan znak za obilježavanje prisustva i odsustva u dokumentaciji o zatvorenicima; fotografije zatvorenika uokvirene su formama samih radova – jedna uskličnikom, druga pravougaonikom. Sve predstave tumačimo jedinstvom sa formalnim svojstvima rada; oblik i tekstura platanā i ramova (materijalni sloj) integrisani su u značenje. Sirova platna koja nemaju originalno slikarsku namjenu, već praktičnu, ponekad i vojnu, zajedno sa čeličnim strukturama koje ih uokviruju, upućuju na brutalističku estetiku sirovine same; umjesto uljepšavanja svjedočimo potrebi da se asocijativnost materije utka u značenje djela. Oblik slike postaje znak, pa i simbol – on upućuje na ključ u kojem se predstava tumači, određuje ugao posmatranja. Fotografije korišćene uvećane i skenirane, ali u svom izvornom stanju, postavljene su u dijalog sa likovnim intervencijama – materijalima, znacima, oblicima, kompozicionim jukstapozicijama, nametnutim okvirima i, naposljetku, na jednom dijelu slike, slikarskim intervencijama umjetnice.

U prisustvu radova, već pri prvom susretu, atmosfera obuzima prostor u kojem su izložene, prostor između slika samih, kao i onaj unutar posmatrača. Nijanse crvene i boje rđe kombinovane sa sivom, te platnima tamnoplave boje, izazivaju osjećaj ozbiljnosti teme. Zrnaste strukture odštampanih uveličanih fotografija povremeno djeluju kao apstraktne kompozicije, a kod *Gateway to the Gulf* (2024) forme se miješaju do neprepoznatljivosti. Utisak neizvjesnosti rađa tenziju. Pri inicijalnom susretu naziremo teme radova: jasne asocijacije daju – rupe od metaka u čeličnom ramu na slici *Gateway to the Gulf* (2024), na skulpturi to je replika okova sa fasade tvrđave *Limb Immobilizer* (2024), na slici *Threshold (Gigantomachy Concerning a Void)* (2024) to je apstraktna mješavina materijala koja podsjeća na otvorenu ranu, te tako opskurna atmosfera i bez predznanja navodi na dalje istraživanje značenja uprkos dozi straha i tihe jeze.

Dominantna tema – odnos prema istorijskom nasljeđu i kolektivnom sjećanju – povlači sa sobom druge važne teme: odnos prema Zlu, uloga u njegovom opstanku, pitanja ljudske i političke odgovornosti prema drugima i prema sjećanju. Valter Benjamin zapaža: „Istorijski artikulisati prošlost ne znači spoznati je *kakva je, u stvari, bila*. To znači ovladati sećanjem onako kako blesne u trenutku opasnosti"[1] . Darja Bajagić ne pretenduje da se upotrebom fotografija iz arhiva bavi pojmom svjedočanstva, ona upravo evocira ovaj trenutak opasnosti kao uvijek moguć. Slike pred nama nijesu sjećanja, to su umjetničke vizije koje koriste istorijske dokaze i podsjećaju na ono što mislimo da smo izbjegli. Susan Sontag kaže kako nema nečeg poput kolektivnog sjećanja, već ima samo individualnog sjećanja i kolektivne instrukcije.[2] Način na koji pamtimo u javnom diskursu istorijske događaje poput stradanja u fašističkim i nacističkim logorima i kako se odnosimo prema njima u velikoj mjeri je određen političkim i ideološkim odnosima moći. No koji god da se zločin pamti ili zaboravlja – princip je isti: „ovi zločinci nismo mi". Istorija se desila u vakuumu datih okolnosti i akterā trenutka, a mi smo, sa dovoljne vremenske distance, njeni nevini svjedoci. Slike iz ove serije subvertiraju ovaj stav. Zlo(čin) se dešava uvijek i svuda.

„Logor je prostor koji se otvara kada stanje izuzeća počinje da postaje pravilo", zaključuje Đorđo Agamben; to je prostor gdje je zakon u cjelosti suspendovan.[3] Logor je upisivanje samog golog života u poredak – „znak nemogućnosti sistema da funkcioniše a da se ne

1   Benjamin, Walter. *Eseji.* 1974. Nolit: Beograd, str. 80

2   Sontag, Susan. *Regarding the Pain of Others*. 2004. Penguin Books, p.74.

3   Ono važno što Agamben ističe o nastanku logora (i u *campos concentraciones* koje su Španci stvorili na Kubi 1896. i *concentration camps* u koje su Englezi strpali Bure početkom 20. v.) jeste da oni nastaju iz stanja izuzeća, u njegovom proširenju na čitavo civilno stanovništvo. (Agamben, 2020)

transformiše u smrtonosnu mašinu“. Implikacija njegovih definicija jeste da je logor utisnut u sâm poredak kao skrivena matrica politike u kojoj i dalje živimo i koju moramo naučiti da prepoznajemo u svim njenim metamorfozama.[4] Bodrijar u knjizi *Transparentnost Zla* iznosi ideju da je u društvu u kojem je nemoguće govoriti o Zlu – Zlo metamorfoziralo u viralnu i terorističku formu koja nas opsijeda. On postavlja pitanje: „Gdje je Zlo otišlo?“ i odgovara: „Svuda.“[5] I Agamben i Bodrijar odlaze od naivne slike svijeta, politike i društva, gdje postoje „žrtve“ i „agresori“, gdje polarizovani pogled na stvarnost sve nas dijeli na „nevine“ i „krive“ upozoravajući na zavodljivost Zla (Neprijatelja) i opasnost od pristupa sa distance, sa tačke moralne ispravnosti. Dok Agamben upozorava da ćemo sa neprijateljem čiju strukturu ne poznajemo prije ili kasnije početi da se identifikujemo, Bodrijar kaže da se protiv Zla mora boriti jednako – Zlom. Ako izgubimo vezu sa Zlom, ako prestanemo sa njim da se identifikujemo, za nas postoje dvije mogućnosti – da bez imuniteta umiremo na najmanji dodir sa svijetom ili da počnemo da ga nesvjesno reprodukujemo.

Bajagić poziva na preispitivanje licemjerja u otklonu od Zla i zločinā, bilo savremenih, bilo istorijskih. Nejasna pozicija subjekta u suočavanju sa onim što se desilo (jer je bilo dozvoljeno da se desi) poziva na odgovornost. Nema nevinih posmatrača. Slike isprva bude jezu i strah, ali potom i bijes, bol i stid. Ako smo i dalje sebe uspjeli da održimo kao moralnog posmatrača, bijes je usmjeren na istorijskog neprijatelja – fašizam, i njegov savremeni ekvivalent – zaborav. Iz bijesa i patnje postavljamo pitanja: kako su takva varvarstva počinjena u 20. vijeku? Ili: kako takve zločine čovjek može da učini čovjeku? Pomenuta dva filozofa ističu licemjerje i naivnost ovakvih pitanja – Agamben rekavši da je pitanje koje treba postaviti zapravo „koje su pravne procedure i dispozitivi moći to omogućili“, a Bodrijar naglašavajući da „varvarstva“ nijesu nekakve iracionalne epizode čovječanstva, već nešto što je u potpunosti u skladu sa društvenim težnjama skoka u ambis. Ako se okanemo licemjerja, dolazimo do tri opcije – patnja, stid i strah, gdje nas stid, bez obzira na poriv, tjera da gledamo i suočimo se, da prihvatimo odgovornost, a strah dozvoljava okretanje glave pred hororima i podstiče distancu sebe i Drugog. Posmatrač takođe uvijek može da se i adaptira. Naviknuti smo da se branimo od uznemirujućeg, da okrećemo glavu od onog što znamo da se dešava i da je užasno. Sa druge strane, ljudi i dalje imaju potrebu da tuguju, budući da je patos kao narativ dublje ukorijenjen u diskursu i da ima iscjeliteljski efekat. Govoreći o gledanju horora i patosa u prikazima stradanja, Sontag piše: „Sve dok osećamo empatiju za patnju drugih, nismo saučesnici u izazivanju patnje.“[6] „Ko ima stomak da gleda – potvrđuje da je patnja spektakl, predviđen za gledanje – što implicira njenu nužnost: ne, patnja ne može biti zaustavljena.“[7] Ona je strašna činjenica, sastavni dio života, ali ne dešava se *meni*. Tu prestaje naša odgovornost, ali i strah – patnja koja se dešava nekom drugom, fizički i istorijski udaljena je, nije prijetnja. Kad smo završili plakanje za hororima svijeta, možemo da nastavimo svoj pravedni život, iskupljeni svojom patnjom za druge. „Ona se meni ne dešava jer ja nisam zaslužila, ja sam dobra.“

Sa jezivim je drugačije. Jezivo ne dozvoljava iscjeljenje, ono poziva da budemo ili posmatrači ili kukavice koji okreću glavu u nemogućnosti da gledaju prizor. Ikonografija patnje prisutna je u radu Darje Bajagić od samog početka, međutim, patnja je uvijek praćena pitoresknim hororom. Zato su slike Darje Bajagić kao minsko polje. Bez uvida u to u koje ishode nas vode, one onemogućavaju impulsivno kretanje u ma kojem pravcu, one pozivaju na strategiju, na samosvijest i promišljanje. Granice između nas i prikazanog, između stvarnosti i fikcije, između istorije i sadašnjice – nijesu jasne, zato bude strah da se Zlo uvlači u realnost, da nas okružuje, da može već biti u nama a da mi ne možemo da ga prepoznamo. Đavo je dobio formu i ona je neizvjesnost i neznanje. „Šta ako sam Zla?“

Ambiguitet pozicije posmatrača koji slike izazivaju stvara anksioznost – pakao našeg vremena. Nemamo dovoljno informacija da znamo jesmo li na pravoj strani i – šta ako greškom

4   Agamben, Đorđo. *Šta je logor?* 2020. Beograd: FMK.

5   Baudrillard, Jean. *Transparency of Evil*. 1993. London: Verso, p.81.

6   Agamben (2020), ibid, 89.

7   Sontag, ibid.

budemo akteri na pogrešnoj? Ne možemo donijeti odluku jer nemamo aparat za slučaj da smo pogriješili, nemamo snage za krivicu ni hrabrosti za odgovornost. Nemamo unaprijed spremljene dokaze sopstvene nevinosti, niti mogućnost da dilemu razriješimo, stoga ostajemo ontološki paralisani u nemogućnosti da budemo bilo šta od ponuđenog – žrtve, agresori, posmatrači (saučesnici), nevini posmatrači.

Pomislilo bi se da u temi poput pretvaranja bivšeg logora u luksuzni hotel nema prostora nijansiranom pogledu na fenomen, ali kod Darje Bajagić je ta siva zona upravo cilj umjetničkog rada. Korak koji ona čini je transgresija u koju se umjetnici ne upuštaju jer savremeno društvo diktira sve polarizovaniji pogled na stvarnost, u kojem postoji određena „prava strana istorije", moralna ispravnost određenog stava koji se ne dovodi u pitanje. Stvarajući radove koji posmatrača dovode u pitanje zajedno sa pogledom na fenomen, Bajagić vraća umjetnosti funkciju poziva na odnos. Ona kolektivno sjećanje i lični odnos prema istoriji preko umjetnosti apstrahuje na metanivo, gdje je manje važno da li, gdje i kada se Zlo dogodilo; ona okreće ogledalo ka unutra – ko smo mi u tom Zločinu, koja osjećanja u nama to izaziva: to je ono što pojedinac neće zaboraviti u odnosu na podatak. Nova epistemologija nije intelektualna, ona je tjelesna i emotivna. Umjetnost prekida suđenje i poziva na gledanje u sebe i preispitivanje sopstvene pozicije, poziva na uključenje, na zastajanje radi promišljanja, na tišinu. Bajagić sofisticirano podsjeća na nijanse, na kompleksnost istorije, na našu ulogu u njenoj savremenosti, na nepostojanje moralne nevinosti. Prepoznavanjem Zla u nama, njegovim nijansiranjem kao kontinuuma umjesto kao „druge strane", uvažavanjem njegove zavodljivosti – otvara se mogućnost njegovog sprečavanja. Tako možemo da „nasleđe ponovo preotmemo od konformizma koji namerava da njime ovlada"[8].

SPISAK LITERATURE:

Agamben, Đorđo. *Šta je logor?* 2020. Beograd: Fakultet za medije i komunikacije.
Agamben, Đorđo. *Homo Sacer.* 2018. Loznica: Karpos.
Agamben, Đorđo. *Ono što ostaje od Auschwitza.* 2008. Zagreb: Antibarbarus.
Benjamin, Walter. *Eseji.* 1974. Beograd: Nolit.
Baudrillard, Jean. *The Transparency of Evil.* 1993. London: Verso.
Sontag, Susan. *Regarding the Pain of Others.* 2004. Penguin Books.

8   Benjamin, ibid.

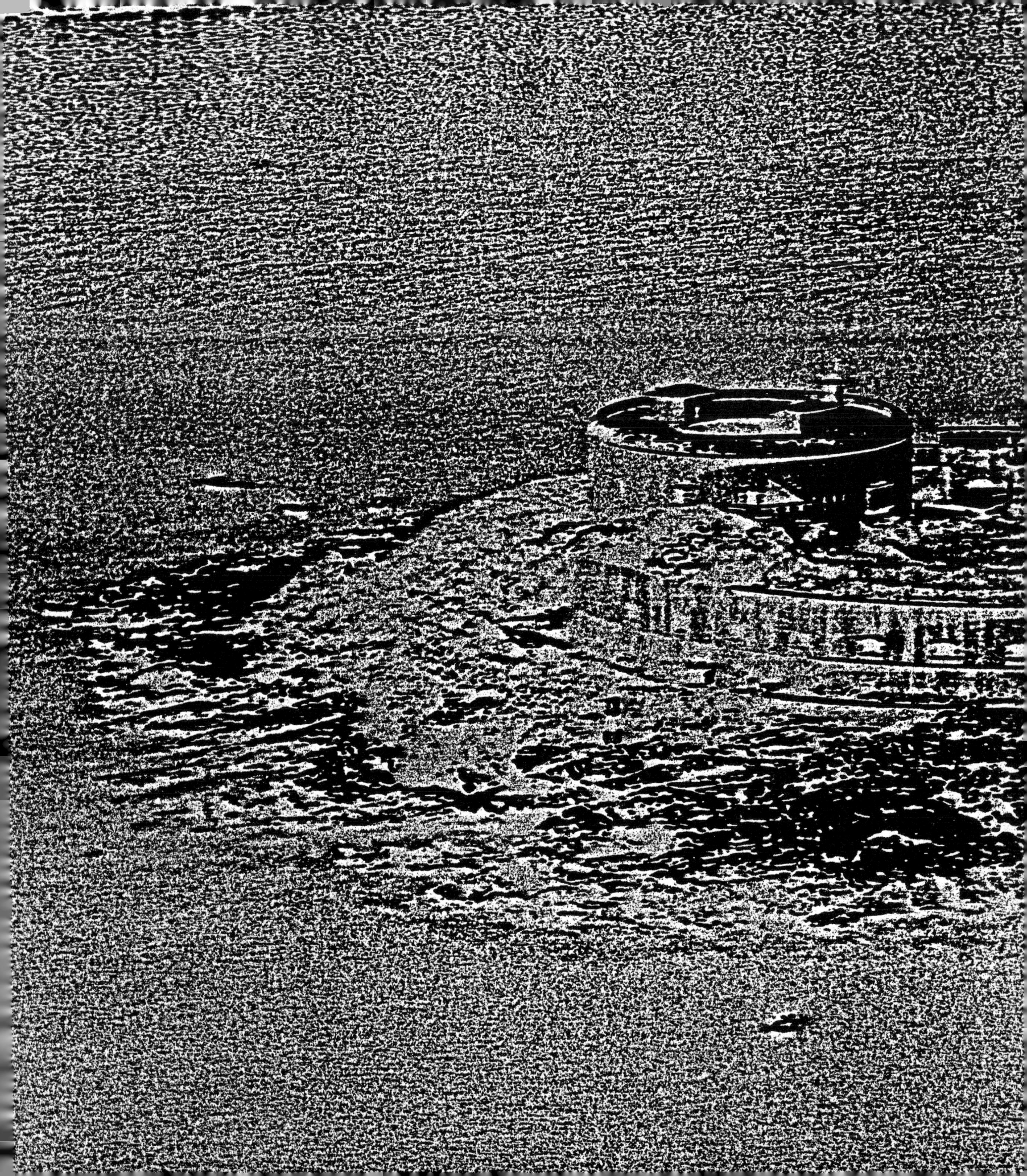

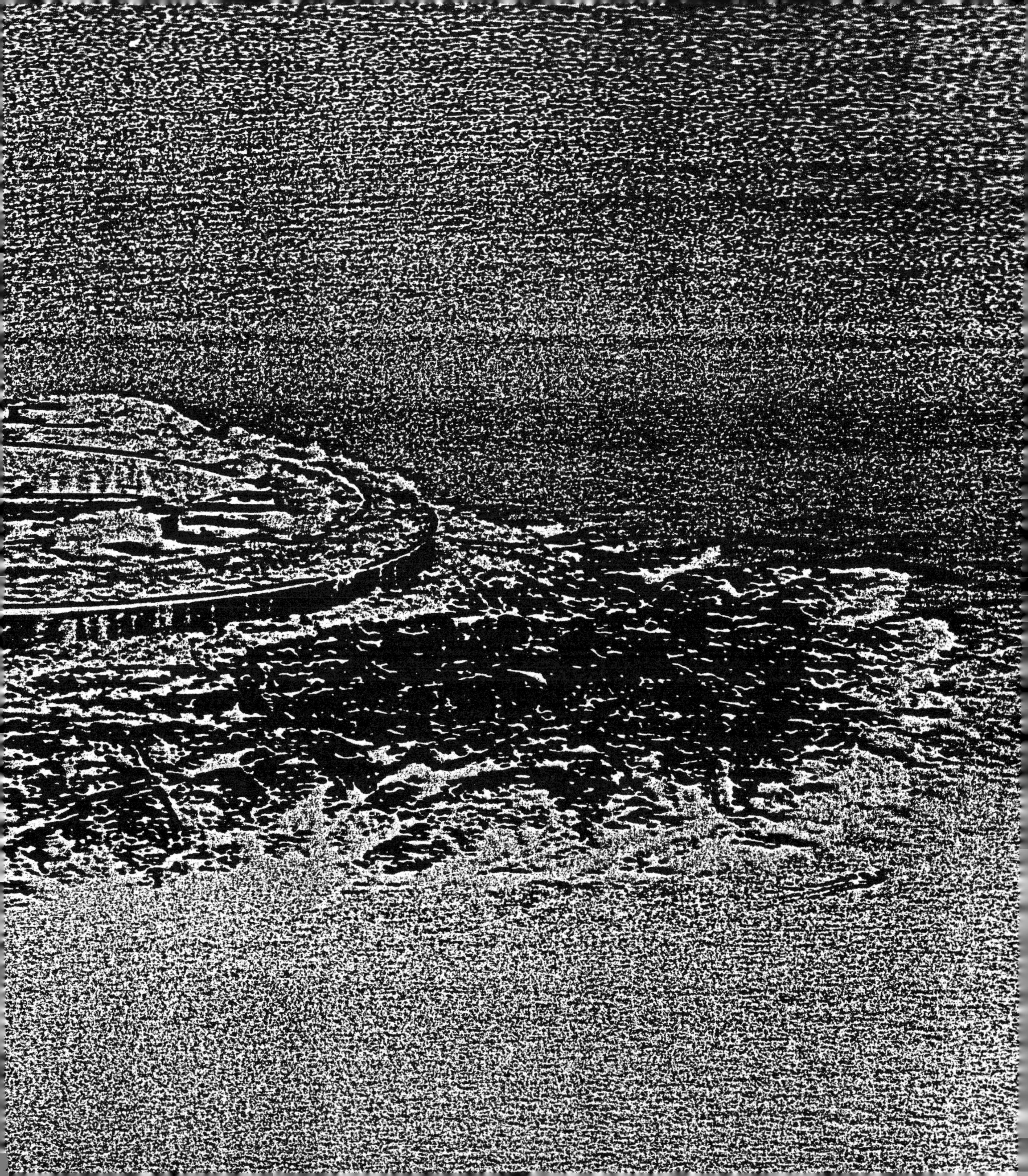

WHAT YOU DON'T SEE IS WHAT YOU MAY GET

Ingrid Luquet-Gad

History returns first as tragedy, then as farce.[1] In the case Darja Bajagić's latest body of works, the farcical nature of eternal return is better understood through its current iteration: history returns as a sanitized, neoliberal limbo. Neither hell nor paradise, it is stuck in a perpetual present; one that has been carefully crafted to seem cool, smooth, and frictionless. To appear as such means that what we see is the result of a deeper process, aimed at a final stage of amnesiac depoliticization. There, the past does not exist, and the future has been suspended. Everything has been reshaped to please the median taste of an international, faceless vacationer: not a subjectivity, just a statistic. Welcome to Mamula Island: a tiny Montenegrin piece of land located in the middle of the Adriatic Sea and the rocky host to an impregnable 19th century fortress occupying almost the entirety of its surface area. Nowadays, the site hosts a luxury hotel whose website proclaims: "The word 'unique' is often overused. It is, however, the best way to describe Mamula Island." If one scrolls further down, a Swiss-style typeface spells out its slogan: "It takes an island to feel this good." We are already aware of how the universal, post-national order of an Empire[2] with no outside encompasses the totality of reality; we are also familiar with how different capitalisms only ever reframe that sole and same reality. And yet, feel-good capitalism has rarely seemed so unapologetic: this is the paradisiac manufacturing of consent,[3] tailored to fit our post-political age. With water so blue that any hard feelings, unsettling facts, or disturbing truths would just float away—wouldn't they?

The tagline now also gives its title to Darja Bajagić's participation in the 60th International Art Exhibition – La Biennale di Venezia, where the artist has been chosen to represent her home country Montenegro. Born in 1990, the artist emigrated as a child and settled in Egypt before arriving in the United States in 1999. In 2021, she relocated to her native country and settled in Luštica Peninsula. From there, she explains, she would see the island looming from afar every day and heard stories about it from several people whose relatives had been to Mamula. That other memory, the embodied one, was kept alive through word-of-mouth; material documentation, however, was sparse and practically non-existent. Bajagić only knew, as most Montenegrins, that the site had a charged historical background. The fort was initially erected in 1863 by the Austro-Hungarian general Lazar Mamula, who gave his name to the premises. Otherwise uninhabited, the piece of land became a part of the Empire's defense plans. Then, during World War II, the fascist forces of Benito Mussolini converted the fort into a concentration camp. From 1942 until the end of the war, its deserted location enabled secrets to be buried, dissensus to be deadened, and forgetfulness to continue being fostered. The last part of the island's official development started in 2015, when the government granted a Switzerland-based development holding permission to convert the former camp into a luxury resort. Privatization began, and the mechanics of glossing over the past were set into motion. Gradu-

1   The much-quoted phrase appears initially as a remark by Karl Marx, commenting on Georg Wilhelm Friedrich Hegel in *The Eighteenth Brumaire of Louis Bonaparte*, 1852. It is also the title of a book by Slavoj Zizek, *First as Tragedy, Then as Farce* (2009): fittingly, he diagnoses the two-fold failure of Western liberalism, first as a political doctrine and then as an economic theory.

2   Michael Hardt & Antonio Negri, Empire (Cambridge: Harvard University Press, 2000).

3   The phrase was popularized by the book *Manufacturing Consent: The Political Economy of the Mass Media* (1988) by Edward S. Herman and Noam Chomsky, where the authors analyze how the modern U.S. government utilizes mass-media to the same ends as violent means of coercion.

ally, in media representation and through the resort's public communication, the camp would be framed as a prison, and the erasure of history would be conflated with a "careful restoration" of the building.[4]

Darja Bajagić returned to Montenegro having established herself internationally as an uncompromising observer of both the symbolic construction and the mediatic circulation of images: the ones hidden and forbidden, and, therefore often also, the ones fetishized and collected. After graduating from Yale University in 2014, her first body of work took pornographic imagery as its source material. Bajagić's treatment of an otherwise post modern theme per excellence[5] related to its specific timeframe and technologically engineered perceptual regime. The artist chose to isolate figures that, already in themselves, eluded such reductive pitfalls as moralistic tales of consumption and objectification, or teleological stories of redemption and salvation.[6] One less explored strand of interpretation of these early works connects their inscription in art history with viewer theory as it emerges over the decade. The reversibility of subject and object positions concerns not only what is depicted but also how one interacts with what is depicted. Especially because of the "degree zero" of the pornographic image, we can read the construction of the painterly image in Darja Bajagić's early works as closely intertwined with what has been framed as "participatory culture"[7] in mass-culture and internet-culture alike. In that sense, a deeper, more all-encompassing politics of spectatorship has always been present in the artist's oeuvre; that is, if one concentrates on the relational structure of the works—how they present their subject as much as what they incidentally represent.

To understand the materiality of such a system of presentation and presentification, one needs to first consider their formal lineage. Trained as a minimalist painter, Bajagić isolates her figures inside a shaped canvas to provide them with a new context of apparition and reception. Geometric shapes further complexify the reading of the figure, flattening the traditional hierarchies between foreground and background; just as the use of colors, frequently in muted tones of black, grey, or red, contribute to opening up a space of correspondences. Utilizing a multilayered process consisting of print and painterly techniques, thin layers of acrylic paint and UV print on canvas leave each part of the process visible. The total impression is never illusionary, and the potential shock-effect is only accidental: a critical mind could very well unweave and unfurl the effects and working mechanics of the painting. That such a possibility is at hand yet rarely received as such only further enhances the brute power of an image, of any image that instinctively tends to supersede the careful consideration of its inner workings.

A POLITICS OF RECEPTION:
PARTICIPATION BEYOND CONTEMPLATION

The participatory framing of spectatorship entails that in Bajagić's works, two figures of the viewer coexist that would otherwise be encountered separately in the mediatic sphere. There is the everyday voyeur, attracted to the effect of an image rather than to the image itself, and the "emancipated spectator,"[8] interested in the constitution of an image beyond canonical art history and pedagogical visual education. Ultimately, a contemporary framing tends to dissociate them, especially if one considers the period of the 2010s: the viewer as a participant or as a user[9] is preferred over the inherited notion of the spectator as an ideal audience, however emancipated. This is made clear in the artists' oeuvre as she engages with a politics of reception; that is, provided that a first step, necessary and unconditional, be respected: an image's right to appear in the common space of visibility and engage with our indecisive gaze without being preemptively

4   The erasure of history and of its troublesome blind-spots also resonates with a more recent iteration of Empire, namely seasteading: This ultra-neoliberal ideology aims to create… permanent dwellings in international waters outside of governmental territory, thus escaping rules and regulations. It is usually seen through structures such as cruise ships, oil platforms, or custom-built floating islands.

5   See, for instance: Jean Baudrillard's frequent referencing of pornography in relation to war, cyberreality, or consumerism. In: *The Consumer Society* (1970); *Simulacra and Simulation* (1981); and various articles, such as *"War Porn,"* in *Journal of Visual Culture*, 5 (1), Apr. 2006.

6   This is exemplified through the artist's recurrent figure of the actress Dominno through works such as *L'Hexagone (Intolerable Dominnation)*, 2019 or *Transfiguration*, 2019: her blank-faced expression, refusing to engage, makes her an open canvas for projection, presentation (for the artist), and reappropriation (for both artist and viewer).

7   The concept of "participatory culture" was explored at length by pioneering works by Henry Jenkins such *Textual Poachers* (1992) or *Fans, Bloggers, and Gamers* (2006).

8   Jacques Rancière, *The Emancipated Spectator* (Paris: Éditions la Fabrique, 2008).

9   See, relating to visual arts in the 2010s more specifically: Stephen Wright, Toward a Lexicon of Usership (Eindhoven: Van Abbemuseum, 2013).

deemed good or bad. Such a precaution particularly applies to a second period in the artist's production: a change in subject matter appears in the second half of the decade, responding to the times' shifting iconographical blind spot. More precisely, the circulated sexual content in the first era of Web 2.0 gave way to the more ominous presence of crime and war imagery. Where the sexual content is *more* than an image, too purely corporeal to be looked at, the sensationalized criminal content—whether extremist iconologies, portraits of mass murderers or of abducted children—is *less* than an image: already hiding in plain sight, even when circulated by the mass media, and therefore not even needing to be hidden anymore.[10]

Over the span of Darja Bajagić's production, it is noteworthy that the artist's core logic has remained similar—expanding, adapting, and deepening. The formal approach kept developing following the same axioms, although the fabrication of duality, necessary to escape the overly referential nature of the source-images, became an increasingly erudite task. In works from that second period,[11] we see how the manipulation of symbols now rendered available through their insertion into circuits of disseminated imagery overtake the global, ahistorical space of a mediatic environment with neither refuge nor respite. In a sense, what has often been postulated as the contextlessness of digital images is precisely countered by a careful reframing of those sources by the artist—for instance, by providing information in her titles. However, this does not mean that they are reattributed to their "authentic" origin, but rather the contrary: their circulation has added to the plurality of sources through various participatory uses and multiple sites of appearance. What the early techno-utopians of the 1990s did get right is that the free web made iconographic literacy accessible to most. After all, extreme-right groups and neo-pagan sects in particular mastered the manipulation of polysemic ancient signs and symbols, just as they did with the intricate semiology of social media. This ultimately adds to the position of an artist such as Bajagić, who minutely researches her sources, tracing most of their various uses and misuses,[12] and more essentially, deflects the one-sided purpose characteristic of any subcultural group or movement—the semiotic aspect of identity-building is true for subcultural groups, political movements, and nation building alike.[13] For the artist, polysemy and duality remain key: the fabrication of uncertainty is the goal of the operation; and this can ultimately be perceived once again as relating to a position of the participant-viewer.

Art escapes bourgeois contemplation but it also eludes its avant-gardist ethos.[14] This leads us a third period in Bajagić's oeuvre, corresponding to the body of works presented in *It Takes an Island to Feel This Good*. With it, the preliminary research process has now moved its sphere of operations from the digital to the physical world yet it still does not substantially differ—the current digital space can hardly be thought of as an "elsewhere" nor as separated from the material world. The works' iconographical content similarly stems from material that originally exists in hidden form and more precisely, obfuscated from the public eye. More specifically, the artist has excavated the sparse archive material relating to the disappearing history of Mamula, especially the period from its existence as a camp. As she was not allowed to scan the photographs directly, Bajagić instead used the xeroxes that she obtained in the works. The restricted access clearly appears as a material trace, as one perceives the poor quality of the scans as well as different clues regarding their provenance, such as various administrative markers, be they stamps or watermarks. Nothing is obfuscated in the image itself, only presented inside a reframing that enables the politics of spectatorship to emerge without the preconditioned perceptual reflexes of everyday life and belief systems. Bajagić has enlarged archival documents and transferred them onto the five canvases that compose the Venetian series. She then treats each canvas with a different shape and color. What emerges through the delineation of a

10   The narrowing and subsequent policing of a free web has been chronicled by Geert Lovink though his investigations into critical internet culture. See the trilogy formed by: *My First Recession* (2003), *Zero Comments* (2008), and *Networks Without a Cause* (2011).

11   Exemplified for instance in the 2018 works *Beate, the stony-faced nymphomaniac power-freak, projecting an aura of normality with Susann* and *Beate – helpful, kind, nice, obliging, primitive, subliminally aggressive and vulgar*.

12   In a previous interview, the artist detailed how she would assemble source-material comprised of "at least twenty pages of research, images and sketches." See: "Darja Bajagić: Save the Art, Kill the Image," in *Spike Art Magazine*, #72, June 2022, pp. 80-91.

13   In his 1993 book *Imagined Communities*, Benedict Anderson shows how media create a sense of community through the power of imagination, particularly through the written word in books, newspapers, and various magazines that he names "print capitalism."

14   The historical avant-gardes' conception of art elaborated in response to the rise of fascism is propagandist in substance: art is essentially responding to a social function (XVI) and needs to be efficient enough to counter the enemy's own "formation of masses" (XIX). See: Walter Benjamin's analysis of film in Walter Benjamin, *The Work of Art in the Age of Its Technological Reproducibility: Second Version, 1935-1939* (Cambridge: Harvard University Press, 1999)

new context of circulation is also a different, alternative framing of an event, thus subtly hinting back to the strategy applied in the real world of Empire. In the case of Mamula's manufacturing of the feel-good present, those multiple possible framings have been narrowed down to one sole and only path. No choice, no problem. Or to put it differently: no freedom, just forever feel-good capitalism.

PORNOGRAPHIC, CRIMINAL, ARCHIVAL:
THREE REGISTERS OF THE IMAGE

In the Pavilion of Montenegro, the exhibition presents the five, steel-framed acrylic and UV printed canvases in dialogue with a sculpture.[15] The iconographical works are alternatively treated in a scale of grey or in a plain, muted background color such as burgundy, rust, or blue. What must be emphasized here is how none of the paintings apply the same iconographic strategy, whether through shapes or colors. They avoid any sense of unification at all, even an alternative one. If one considers the series from the standpoint of reception, the motives themselves are imbued with a silent quality, and a first encounter with this new kind of hidden iconographic material leaves one at a loss for words: the deep-seated, typically swift reflex of approval or condemnation, acquired through social media's "like button" paradigm, is derailed as perceptual reflexes must be relearned so as to leave space for nuance. All slightly bigger than human size, the works are hung low and supplemented with a sculpture anchoring their reception in physical space, and not only iconographical, context. Thus, a cast iron ankle holder rematerializes in the exhibition space, which references the ones used for captives. Formerly sprinkled around Mamula, they have now been removed and only subsist, like all the source material, through their vanishing traces on a carefully restricted photograph.

Submerged by the scale of the paintings, which bear little reference to the world as it presents itself to natural perception, we start to feel lost in a totality of grainy, disappearing motives as well as stubborn shapes and colors that now, more than ever in the artist's oeuvre, verge on the purely geometrical. Such a framing of the archive is one that displaces the truth-value that one tends to automatically assign to a historical document, any historical document, and particularly to one that relates to war crimes and stories of imprisonment. What Bajagić achieves through this ensemble is to show how an archival source tends to exert an unquestionable authority on the viewer, however much it has been distorted, reworked, and set into motion through another system of perception as well a different context of circulation and apparition. Conversely, the ensemble also hints at how the viewer, here as well, can regain their critical position in front of an image to reinterrogate how historically constructed perceptions operate on us and ultimately shape our reception when presented with a narrative, explanation, or theory. Neither pathos nor horror will save us from having to make a choice for ourselves.

Pornographic image, criminal image, archival image: inside her system, the artist reworks the three main registers of the contemporary image to carefully craft the conditions of a fragile suspension of (dis)belief. There is however a distinction to be established between those three regimes of the image. The pornographic, the criminal, and the archival image also correspond, in their reworking by the artist, to the specific techno-mediatic paradigm within which they are circulated. Namely, the archival image also demands to be read amidst the current tendency for abstraction to be perceived as a marker of truth, at the same time as transparency, conversely, is now being cast under the suspicion of turning oppressive. One of the most obvious examples of this shift is best observed through an artistic paradigm that was widespread at the turn of the last decade, ultimately conveying a belief in the emancipatory nature of non-visibility and

15   For the paintings: Darja Bajagić, *The Murder of the Sign*; *Frustum — Numero 11: Komadat Logora Mamula (Piece of Mamula Camp)* or *Komandat Logora Mamula (Commander of Mamula Camp*; *Threshold (Gigantomachy Concerning a Void)*; *Gateway to the Gulf*; *The Ambivalence of the Sacred*, all 2024. For the sculpture: Darja Bajagić, *Limb Immobilizer (Iron Rings to Which Some Prisoners Were Tied)*, 2024.

29

in the intrinsic values of "not being seen."[16] Others, in a less simplistic fashion perhaps, have pointed to the abstraction inherent in machine vision, surveillance systems, and data extraction patterns alike,[17] or have articulated the "concrete and causal relationship between the complexity of the systems we encounter every day; the opacity with which most of those systems are constructed or described; and fundamental, global issues of inequality, violence, populism and fundamentalism."[18]

BEYOND TRUTH, PROOF, IDENTIFICATION,
AND FACT-CHECKING

As subjects of mainstream 21st media culture, we are faced with the need to unlearn our blind trust in the image as proof and to begin moving away from the inherent truth-value we inevitably tend to attach to the historical document. One needs only consider the proliferation of hyper-graphic war images in our social-media news feeds, that eerie space where self-commodification blends with a general abstraction of the real, where all types of imagery come together and blend in a flood of images with no origin, images unmoored from any real coordinates, that is, the now fully generated images of artificial intelligence. This also entails that a representation that is too graphic, too precise, or too detailed immediately becomes suspicious: it is this kind of imagery, previously hidden (*true because hidden*), that has now become suspicious (*dubious because exposed*). Bajagić still has no interest in unveiling any truth, nor to cultivate any belief in its iconographic existence; rather, she keeps making us, the viewer, face the grey zone, where we will, ultimately, again and again, need to decide for ourselves, or to choose, but only after a process of unlearning, not to decide at all.

Our present time tasks us with reexamining the truth-value of archives. However, nowhere is this inherent attribution of value more evident that in the art world's blind faith therein.[19] At the beginning of the 21st century, a quasi-religious faith in the image as proof is shining brighter than ever and this especially manifests in the archival document, through the array of practices that have now turned to looking for a core truth in the molecular, atomic pores of the real. For several of those artist-seekers, truth-value has been rekindled: it is there but we just can't see it, meaning that a perfecting of new technological tools would lead us to a definitive unveiling. The question of mechanical vision and its relation to reality is not new. Walter Benjamin already contrasted two conceptual characters: the magician and the surgeon, which corresponded to the painter and to the cameraman. To him, the latter "penetrates deep into the subject's tissue,"[20] and from a pre-digital visual environment, already works from fragments and edits, alters the duration of time, space, and points of view. The relation one can draw to our present time is not explicit, but it can however be seen to mark the beginning of our current algorithmically engineered content-production: we now look for an origin in the invisible pores of the real. Thus, it is not truth value that has been abandoned, but its search that has been expanded.

Truth, proof, identification, fact-checking;[21] image recognition techniques, open-source intelligence tools, cultural analytics:[22] those are the current paradigms of the 2020s with and against which Darja Bajagić's new body of work must be read. The Mamula ensemble presented at the 60th International Art Exhibition – La Biennale di Venezia indicates a furthering of the iconographical regimes that make up the totality of her oeuvre by adding a third one, the archival, to the two existing ones, showing how her artistic system can encompass the shifting nature of mediatic circulation and of the viewer-participant's belief systems. Here, while the new mediatic environment runs parallel to the artist's own progression, Bajagić's iconological sources, aesthetic strat-

16   The theme of protesting and subverting facial recognition is recurrent in the works and writings from the 2010s by artists such as Hito Steyerl or Zach Blas.

17   See for instance, the works of Trevor Paglen.

18   James Bridle, *New Dark Age* (London: Verso Books, 2018), 12

19   A thorough analysis of this phenomenon is provided by Claire Bishop in her article "Information Overload," *Artforum*, 61 (80), Apr, 23.

20   Benjamin, *Op. Cit.*, XIV.

21   See for instance the practice of Forensic Architecture in general for images; and Lawrence Abu Hamdan in general for sound.

22   Lev Manovich, *Cultural Analytics*, 2020.

egies, and spectatorship politics can also be read through how this system differs in relation to this strand of practices and their implied framings of the real. Inside Empire, or its metonymic approach through the Mamula series, there is no community left, and therefore also no interpretative community to refer back to. In a neoliberal global world order, forever cool, always smooth, and above all atomized in its individualist social configuration, participatory spectatorship can still exist as a guiding principle, but it must at the same time be reframed as a radically solitary endeavor: the group-effect which previously gave ideology or religion their soothing solace is long gone. The neoliberal limbo only exacerbates the weight of perceptual freedom that Darja Bajagić extends to us here: it is a freedom, but one that doesn't feel like a liberation, double-edged and as heavy on the limbs as an ankle holder. What we can gain from such an act of iconographic and semiotic unlearning is one that will leave us in the throes of freedom and faced with the existential dread of choice. If, however, we chose to play along, well conscious of what we take on by accepting the weight; if we accept to enter the show and spend time in that suspended space of sensorial reconfiguration, we might be freed from the enduring allure of false algorithmic certainties. It really does take an island.

The neoliberal limbo only exacerbates the
weight of perceptual freedom that Darja Bajagić
extends to us here: it is a freedom, but one that
doesn't feel like a liberation, double-edged and
as heavy on the limbs as an ankle holder. What
we can gain from such an act of iconographic
and semiotic unlearning is one that will leave
us in the throes of freedom and faced with the
existential dread of choice.

Neoliberalni limb samo povećava težinu
perceptivne slobode koju nam Darja Bajagić ovdje
pruža: to je sloboda, ali ne liči na oslobođenje, sa
dvije oštrice i teška za udove kao okov za gležanj.
Iz takvog čina ikonografskog i semiotičkog
odučavanja možemo dobiti ono što će nas ostaviti
na mukama slobode i suočiti sa egzistencijalnim
strahom od izbora.

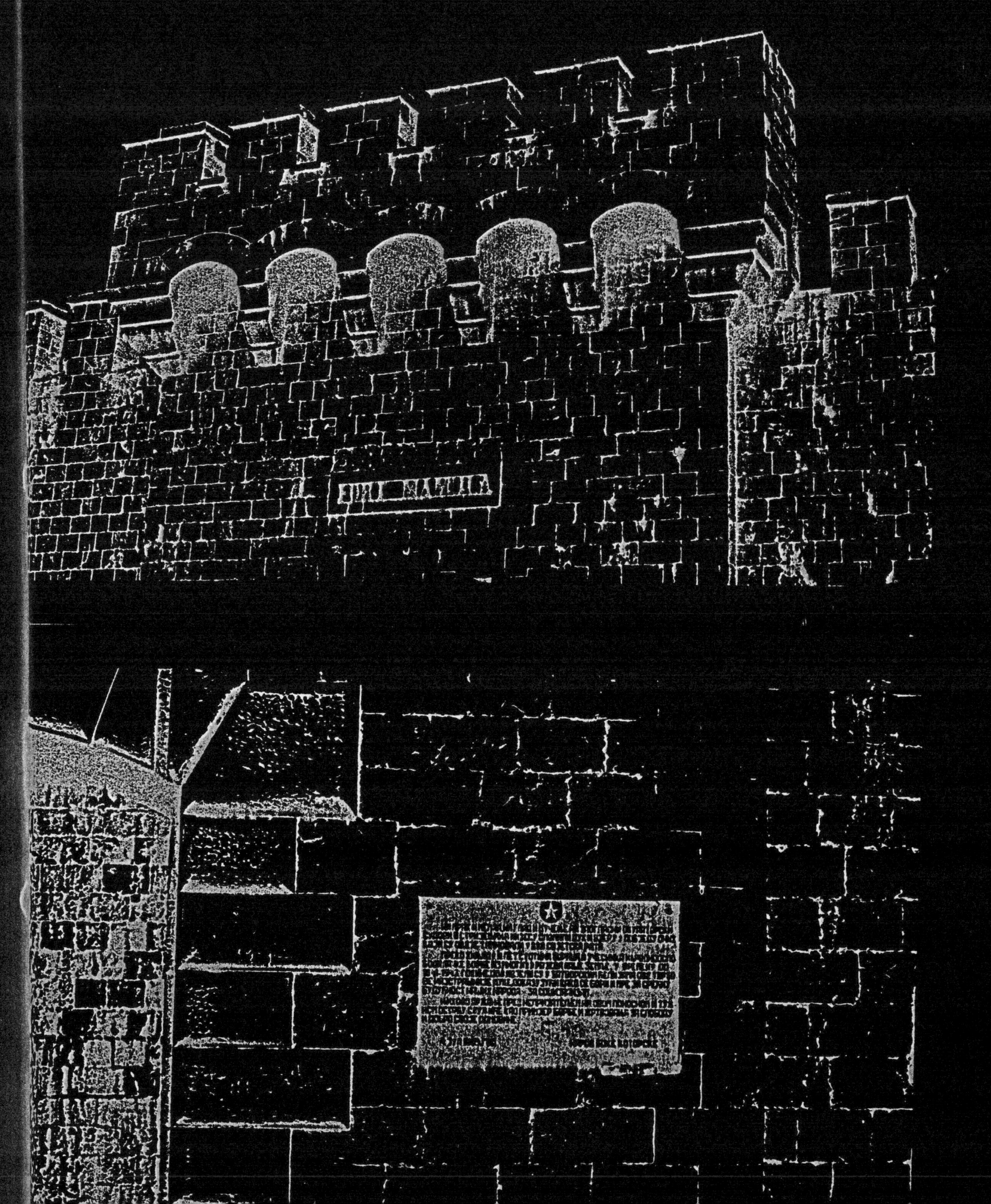

ONO ŠTO NE VIDIŠ JE ONO ŠTO ĆEŠ MOŽDA DOBITI

Ingrid Luquet-Gad

Istorija se prvo ponavlja kao tragedija, onda kao farsa.[1] U slučaju najnovijeg opusa radova Darje Bajagić, farsična priroda vječitog ponavljanja bolje se razumije pomoću njegove trenutne iteracije: istorija se ponavlja kao sanirani, neoliberalni limb. Nije ni pakao ni raj, već zaglavljena u vječnoj sadašnjosti; sadašnjosti brižljivo skrojenoj da izgleda hladna, uglađena i lišena trzavica. To što nam ona tako izgleda znači da je to što vidimo posljedica dubljeg procesa, usmjerenog ka završnoj fazi amnezijske depolitizacije. Tamo prošlost ne postoji, a budućnost je odložena. Sve je preoblikovano da zadovolji prosječni ukus međunarodnog bezličnog turiste: nije subjektivnost, samo statistika. Dobro došli na ostrvo Mamula: mali crnogorski potez zemlje smješten usred Jadranskog mora i stjenoviti dom neosvojive tvrđave iz 19. vijeka koja zauzima tobožnju cjelost njegove površine. Danas se na tom mjestu nalazi luksuzni hotel na čijem sajtu piše: „Riječ 'jedinstveno' se često previše koristi. Njome se, međutim, ostrvo Mamula najbolje može opisati." Ako se skroluje dolje, fontom koji je naizgled švajcarski – napisana je krilatica: „Potrebno je ostrvo za ovako dobar osjećaj." Već smo svjesni kako univerzalni, postnacionalani poredak Imperije[2] bez spoljašnjosti obuhvata cjelokupnu stvarnost; takođe nam je poznato kako raznorazni kapitalizmi samo preoblikuju tu jednu te istu stvarnost. Pa ipak, kapitalizam zadovoljstva rijetko izgleda nepomirljiv: to je rajska proizvodnja pristanka,[3] skrojena po mjeri našeg postpolitičkog doba. Kada je voda toliko plava, svaka ljutnja, potresna činjenica ili uznemirujuća istina jednostavno bi otplutale – zar ne?

Krilatica sada služi i kao naslov za učešće Darje Bajagić na 60. Međunarodnoj izložbi umjetnosti – La Biennale di Venezia, gdje je izabrana da predstavlja svoju rodnu Crnu Goru. Rođena 1990. godine, umjetnica je kao dijete emigrirala u Egipat, gdje je i odrasla, da bi zatim kao tinejdžerka stigla u Sjedinjene Države. Godine 2021. vratila se u svoju rodnu zemlju i nastanila na poluostrvu Luštica. Odatle je, objašnjava, svakodnevno viđala ostrvo kako se nazire izdaleka i slušala priče o ostrvu od mnogih ljudi čiji su rođaci bili u Mamuli. Ta druga uspomena, ovaploćena, održavala se u životu usmenim predanjem; međutim, materijalna dokumentacija je bila oskudna i bezmalo nepostojeća. Mjesto je, znala je Bajagić, kao i većina Crnogoraca, imalo nabijenu istorijsku pozadinu. Tvrđavu je, 1863. godine, podigao austrougarski general Lazar Mamula, po kome je građevina i dobila ime. Inače naseljen, taj potez zemlje postao je dio odbrambenih planova Carstva. Zatim, za vrijeme Drugog svjetskog rata, fašističke snage Benita Musolinija pretvorile su tvrđavu u koncentracioni logor. Od 1942. do kraja rata njena napuštena lokacija omogućavala je da se tajne zakopavaju, neslaganje guši, a zaborav i dalje njeguje. Posljednji dio zvaničnog razvoja ostrva počeo je 2015. godine, kada je vlada dala dozvolu holding kompaniji sa sjedištem u Švajcarskoj da nekadašnji logor pretvori u luksuzno odmaralište. Privatizacija je počela i pokrenula se mehanika zataškavanja prošlosti. Postepeno,

1   Ta često citirana rečenica najprije se pojavljuje kao primjedba Karla Marksa, opaska na Georga Vilhelma Fridriha Hegela u *Osamnaestom brimeru Luja Bonaparte*, 1852. Ona je ujedno i naslov knjige Slavoja Žižeka, *Prvo kao tragedija, onda kao farsa*, 2009: prikladno, on dijagnosticira dvostruki neuspjeh zapadnog liberalizma, najprije kao političke doktrine, a zatim kao ekonomske teorije.

2   Majkl Hart i Antonio Negri, *Imperija*, 2000.

3   Frazu je popularizovala knjiga *Proizvodnja pristanka: politička ekonomija masovnih medija*, 1988, Edvarda S. Hermana i Noama Čomskog, gdje autori analiziraju kako moderna američka vlada koristi masovne medije u iste svrhe kao sredstva prinude.

u medijskoj reprezentaciji hotela i u njihovoj komunikaciji sa javnošču, logor će polako prerasti u zatvor, a brisanje istorije se stopiti s „pažljivom restauracijom" zgrade.[4]

Darja Bajagić se vratila u Crnu Goru nakon što se međunarodno afirmisala kao nepokolebljiva posmatračica simboličke konstrukcije, ali i medijske cirkulacije slika: onih skrivenih i zabranjenih, i stoga često i onih fetišizovanih i sakupljanih. Nakon što je 2014. godine diplomirala na Univerzitetu Jejl, njen prvi rad uzeo je pornografske slike kao izvorni materijal. Tretman Bajagić te inače par ekselans postmoderne teme u umjetnosti[6] povezan je s njenim osobenim vremenskim okvirom i tehnološki konstruisanim perceptivnim režimom. Umjetnica je odlučila da izoluje figure koje su, već same po sebi, izbjegavale takve reduktivne zamke kao što su potrošnja i objektivizacija moralističkih priča ili teleološke priče o iskupljenju i spasenju.[6] Jedan manje istraženi tok tumačenja tih ranijih radova povezuje njihovo upisivanje u istoriju umjetnosti s teorijom posmatrača koja se pojavljuje tokom te decenije. Reverzibilnost pozicija subjekta i objekta ne tiče se samo onoga što je prikazano, već i načina na koji neko opšti sa onim što je prikazano. Pogotovo zbog „nulte tačke" pornografske slike, konstrukciju slikarske predstave u ranim radovima Darje Bajagić možemo čitati kao tijesno isprepletanu sa onim što je uokvireno kao „kultura participacije"[7] kako u masovnoj, tako i u internet kulturi. U tom smislu, u umjetničinom opusu oduvijek je bila prisutna dublja, sveobuhvatnija politika posmatranja; to jest, ako se usredsrijedimo na relacionu strukturu radova – to kako oni predstavljaju svoj predmet koliko i ono što predstavljaju uzgredno.

Da bi se razumjela materijalnost takvog sistema prezentacije i aktualizacije, najprije treba razmotriti njihovo formalno porijeklo. Školovana kao minimalistička slikarka, Bajagić svoje figure izoluje unutar oblikovanog platna kako bi im pružila novi kontekst pojavljivanja, a time i recepcije. Čitanje figure dodatno komplikuju geometrijski oblici, sravnjujući tradicionalne hijerarhije između prednjeg plana i pozadine, isto kao što upotreba boja, nerijetko u prigušenim tonovima crne, sive ili crvene, doprinosi otvaranju prostora korespondencije. Primjenom višeslojnog pristupa koji se sastoji od tehnika štampanja i slikarstva, tanki slojevi akrilne boje i UV štampe na platnu ostavljaju svaki dio procesa vidljivim. Ukupni utisak nikada nije iluzoran, a potencijalni efekat šoka je samo slučajan: kritični um bi vrlo lako mogao da resplete i otkrije efekte i mehaniku dejstva slike. To što je mogućnost dostupna, ali se rijetko prihvata kao takva, samo dodatno pojačava grubu moć slike, svake slike koja instinktivno teži da potisne pažljivo razmatranje njenog unutrašnjeg djelovanja.

POLITIKA RECEPCIJE:
PARTICIPACIJA VAN KONTEMPLACIJE

Participativno uokvirivanje gledališta podrazumijeva da u djelima Bajagić istovremeno postoje dvije figure posmatrača na koje bismo inače naišli odvojeno u medijskoj sferi. Tu su svakodnevni voajer, privučen efektom slike, a ne samom slikom, i „emancipovani posmatrač",[8] koga zanima konstituisanje slike van kanonske istorije umjetnosti i pedagoškog vizuelnog obrazovanja. Naposljetku, savremeno uokvirivanje teži da ih razdvoji, posebno ako se u obzir uzme razdoblje 2010-ih: posmatrač kao učesnik ili korisnik[9] ima prednost u odnosu na naslijeđenu predstavu o posmatraču kao idealnoj publici, ma koliko emancipovana bila. To je jasno predočeno u umjetničinom opusu kada se ona bavi politikom recepcije; to jest, pod uslovom da se poštuje prvi, neophodan i bezuslovan korak: pravo slike da se pojavi u zajedničkom prostoru vidljivosti i bavi našim neodlučnim pogledom, a da se unaprijed ne smatra dobrom ili lošom. Takva mjera predostrožnosti naročito važi za drugo razdoblje u umjetničinoj produkciji: promjena u temi javlja se u drugoj polovini decenije i odgovara promjeni ikonografske slijepe mrlje vremena. Tačnije, seksualni sadržaj koji je cirkulisao

4   Brisanje istorije i njenih problematičnih slijepih tačaka takođe rezonuje s novijom iteracijom Imperije odnosno sistedingom: dotična ultraneoliberalna ideologija ima za cilj stvaranje stalnih prebivališta u međunarodnim vodama van državnih teritorija, tako izvrdavajući pravila i propise. Obično se vidi u strukturama kao što su kruzeri, naftne platforme ili plutajuća ostrva napravljena po mjeri.

5   Vidi, na primjer: kako Žan Bodrijar često pominje pornografiju u vezi s ratom, kiber-stvarnošću ili konzumerizmom. *U Potrošačkom društvu*, 1970; *Simulakrumima i simulaciji*, 1981. i raznim člancima kao što je „Pornografija rata" u *Journal of Visual Culture*, 5 (1), april 2006.

6   Primjer za to što umjetnica ponavlja figuru glumice Dominno u djelima kao što su *L'Hexagone (Intolerable Dominnation)*, 2019. ili *Transfiguration*, 2019.: sa bezbojnim izrazom lica i odbijanjem da se angažuje, ona postaje otvoreno platno za projekciju, prezentaciju (za umjetnicu) i ponovno prisvajanje (i za umjetnicu i za gledaoca).

7   Pojam „kulture participacije" naširoko se istražuje u pionirskim radovima Henrija Dženkinsa kao što su *Kradljivci teksta*, 1992. ili *Obožavaoci, blogeri i gejmeri*, 2006.

8   Žak Ransije, *Emancipovani gledalac*, 2008.

9   Konkretnije u vezi s likovnim umjetnostima 2010-ih, vidi: Stiven Rajt, *Prema riječniku korisništva*, 2013.

u prvoj eri Veba 2.0 ustupio je mjesto zlokobnijem prisustvu prizora zločina i rata. Dok je seksualni sadržaj *više* od slike, previše čisto tjelesan da bi bio gledan, senzacionalizovani kriminalni sadržaj – bilo da su posrijedi ekstremističke ikonologije, portreti masovnih ubica ili otete djece – jeste *manje* od slike: već se krije naočigled svima, čak i kada ga šire masovni mediji, pa otud više i ne mora da se krije.[10]

Tokom trajanja stvaralačkog perioda Darje Bajagić važno je napomenuti da je osnovna logika umjetnice ostala slična – uz proširivanje, prilagođavanje i produbljivanje. Formalni pristup je nastavio da se razvija shodno istim načelima, iako je izmišljanje dualnosti nužno da bi se izbjegla previše referentna priroda izvornih slika sve više postajalo eruditski zadatak. U djelima iz tog drugog razdoblja[11] vidimo kako manipulacija simbolima (koji su sada dostupni u njihovom umetanju u krugove cirkulisanih slika) preuzima globalni, istorijski prostor medijskog okruženja bez utočišta i predaha. U izvjesnom smislu, ono što se često postulira kao beskontekstnost digitalnih slika precizno se suprotstavlja pažljivim preoblikovanjem tih izvora od strane umjetnice – na primjer, davanjem informacija u nazivima dijela. Međutim, to ne znači da im se ponovo pripisuje njihovo „izvorno" porijeklo, već naprotiv, da je njihova cirkulacija doprinijela mnogostrukosti izvora posredstvom različitih participativnih upotreba i više mjesta pojavljivanja. Ono što su rani tehnoutopisti iz 1990-ih ipak shvatili jeste da je besplatni veb zaista zaslužan za to što je ikonografska pismenost postala dostupna svima. Na kraju krajeva, ekstremno desničarske grupe ili neopaganske sekte, a pogotovo one, postale su majstori poigravanja višeznačnošću drevnih znakova i simbola, kao što su to činili i sa zamršenom semiologijom društvenih medija. To na kraju doprinosi poziciji umjetnice kao što je Bajagić, koja podrobno istražuje svoje izvore, prateći većinu njihovih različitih upotreba i zloupotreba[12] i, što je još važnije, odbacuje jednostranu svrhu svojstvenu svakoj supkulturnoj grupi ili pokretu – semiotički dio građenja identiteta isto tako važi i za supkulturne grupe, političke pokrete i izgradnju nacije.[13] Za umjetnicu višeznačnost i dualnost ostaju ključne: cilj operacije je proizvodnja neizvjesnosti; i to se naposljetku može još jednom shvatiti kao vezano za poziciju učesnika-posmatrača.

Umjetnost izmiče buržoaskoj kontemplaciji, ali i svom avangardističkom etosu.[14] To nas dovodi do trećeg razdoblja u opusu Bajagić, koji odgovara korpusu radova predstavljenih u *Potrebno je ostrvo za ovako dobar osjećaj.* Njime je proces preliminarnog istraživanja sada pomjerio svoju sferu djelovanja iz digitalnog u fizički svijet, ali se još suštinski ne razlikuje – na sadašnji digitalni prostor teško da se može gledati kao na „drugo mjesto", a ne može se gledati ni kao na odvojen od materijalnog svijeta. Slično, ikonografski sadržaj radova proizilazi iz materijala koji prvobitno postoji skriven, tačnije – zamagljen u odnosu na oči javnosti. Tačnije, umjetnica je iskopala oskudan arhivski materijal koji se odnosi na istoriju Mamule koja nestaje, posebno na razdoblje njenog postojanja kao logora. Kako joj nije bilo dozvoljeno da fotografije skenira neposredno, Bajagić se umjesto toga u radovima služila fotokopijama koje je nabavila. Ograničeni pristup se jasno pojavljuje kao materijalni trag jer se uočavaju loš kvalitet skeniranja i različiti tragovi njegovog porijekla – razne administrativne oznake, bilo da su to pečati ili vodeni žigovi. Na samoj slici ništa nije zamućeno, samo predstavljeno u novom okviru koji omogućava da se politika gledanja pojavi bez preduslovljenih perceptivnih refleksa svakodnevnog života i sistema vjerovanja. Bajagić je uvećala arhivske dokumente i prenijela ih na ukupno pet platana komponujući venecijansku seriju, da bi zatim svako platno tretirala u različitim, osobenim oblicima i bojama. Ono što se pojavljuje opisivanjem novog konteksta cirkulacije takođe je drugačije, smještanje događaja u drugačiji okvir, čime se suptilno nagovještava strategija primijenjena u stvarnom svijetu Imperije. U slučaju proizvodnje prijatne sadašnjosti na Lastavici, ti višestruki mogući okviri suženi su na tek jedan jedini put. Nema izbora, nema problema. Ili, drugim riječima: nema slobode, samo zauvijek kapitalizam zadovoljstva.

10   Sužavanje i naknadno praćenje besplatnog veba zabeležio je Gert Lovink u svojim istraživanjima o kritičnoj internet kulturi. Vidi trilogiju koju čine: *Moja prva recesija*, 2003; *Nula komentara*, 2008; *Mreže bez razloga*, 2011.

11   Primjer za to bi mogli bi da budu radovi iz 2018. *Beate, the stony-faced nymphomaniac power-freak, projecting an aura of normality with Susann* i *Beate – helpful, kind, nice, obliging, primitive, subliminally aggressive and vulgar.*

12   U jednom prethodnom intervjuu umjetnica je detaljno opisala kako će sastaviti izvorni materijal koji se sastoji od „najmanje dvadeset stranica istraživanja, slika i skica". Vidi: „Darja Bajagić: sačuvaj umjetnost, ubij sliku", u *Spike Art Magazine*, #72, jun 2022, str. 80–91.

13   U svojoj knjizi *Zamišljenje zajednice* iz 1993. Benedikt Anderson pokazuje kako mediji stvaraju utisak zajednice pomoću moći mašte – u ovom slučaju, posebno pisanom riječju posredstvom knjiga, novina i raznih časopisa koje on naziva „štampanim kapitalizmom".

14   Koncepcija umjetnosti istorijskih avangardi razrađena je kao odgovor na uspon fašizma, koji je u suštini propagandistički: umjetnost u suštini odgovara na društvenu funkciju (XVI) i treba da bude toliko efikasna da se suprotstavi „formaciji masa" samog neprijatelja (XIX). Vidi: analiza filma Valtera Benjamina u *Umjetničko delo u doba njegove tehnološke reproduktivnosti: druga verzija*, 1935–1939.

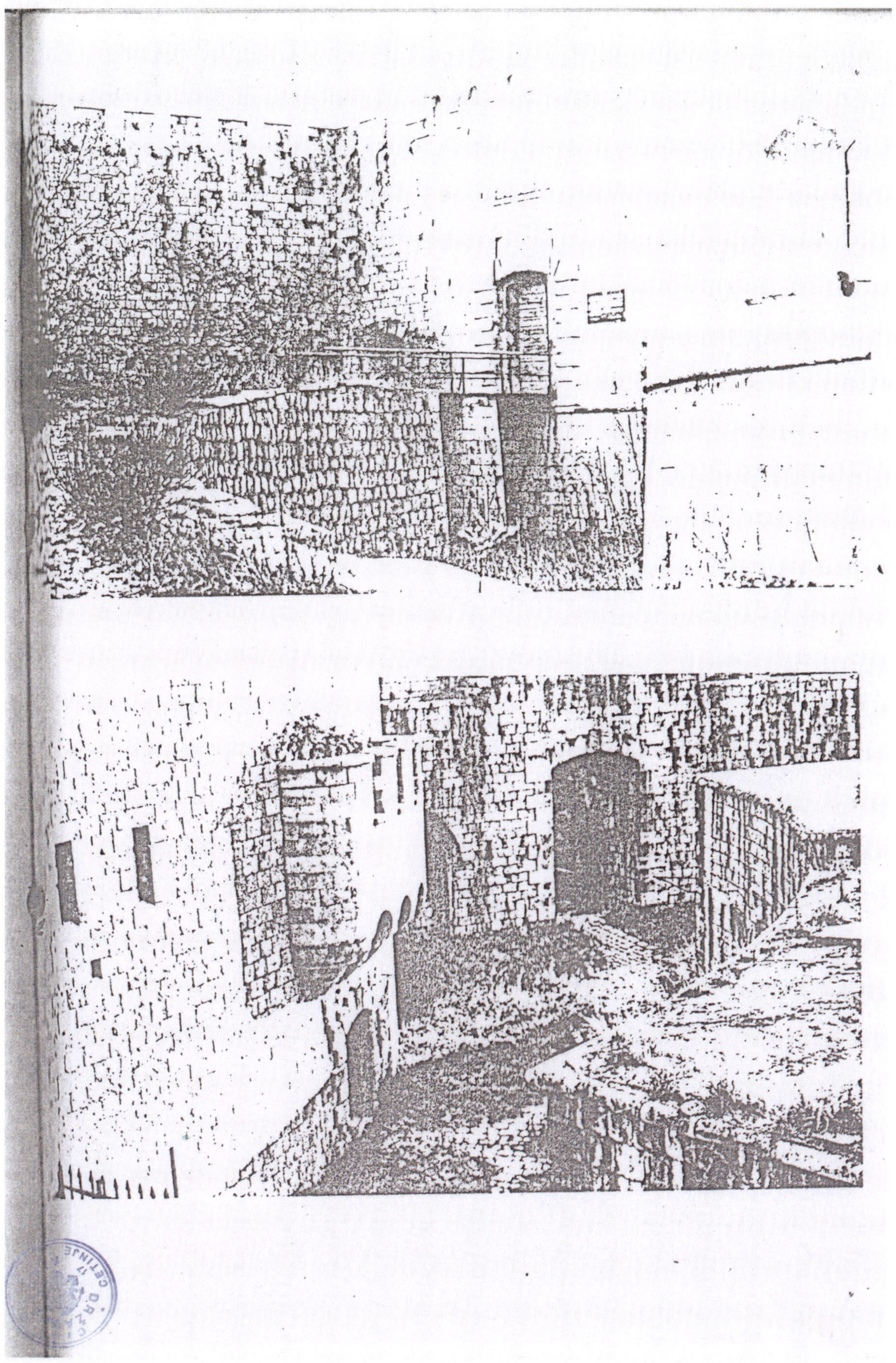

Scan of a photocopy of a document
with an undated photograph of Mamula
island from the State Archives of Montenegro (research material of the artist).

Sken fotokopije dokumenta sa nedatiranom fotografijom ostrva Mamula iz
Državnog arhiva Crne Gore (istraživački
materijal umjetnice).

U paviljonu Crne Gore na izložbi se predstavlja pet čelično uokvirenih akrilnih i UV štampanih platnā predstavljenih u dijalogu sa skulpturom.[15] Ikonografska djela su alternativno obrađena u sivoj skali ili u običnoj, prigušenoj boji pozadine kao što su bordo, boja rđe ili plava. Ovdje se mora podvući kako nijedna slika ne primjenjuje istu ikonografsku strategiju, bilo kroz oblike, bilo kroz boje, izbjegava svako objedinjavanje, pa i alternativno. Ako se serija posmatra iz ugla recepcije, sami motivi su prožeti svojstvom tišine, a prvi susret s tom novom vrstom skrivenog ikonografskog materijala ostavlja bez riječi: duboko ukorijenjeni, uobičajeni brzi refleks odobravanja ili osude, naučen kroz paradigmu „tastera *like*" na društvenim mrežama, izbačen je iz kolosijeka jer se perceptivni refleksi moraju naučiti iznova kako bi se ostavio prostor za nijanse. Jedva nešto veći od čovjekove prirodne veličine, radovi su okačeni nisko i dopunjeni skulpturom koja učvršćuje njihov prijem u fizičkom prostoru, a ne samo u ikonografskom kontekstu. Tako se u izložbenom prostoru ponovo materijalizuje okov za gležanj od livenog gvožđa i ukazuje na one koji su se koristili za zatvorenike. Mamula je ranije bila prošarana njima, ali sada su oni uklonjeni i opstaju, kao i sav izvorni materijal, samo u tragovima koji nestaju na pažljivo ograničenoj fotografiji.

Uronjeni u razmjere slika koje slabo upućuju na svijet onakav kakvim se otkriva prirodnoj percepciji, počinjemo da se osjećamo izgubljeno u totalitetu zrnastih motiva koji nestaju, kao i tvrdoglavih oblika i boja koji se, više no ikada u umjetničinom opusu, graniče sa čisto geometrijskim. Smještanje arhive u takav okvir izmiješta vrijednost istine koja se obično automatski pripisuje istorijskom dokumentu, svakom istorijskom dokumentu, a posebno nekom koji se odnosi na ratne zločine i priče o utamničenju. Bajagić ovim opusom uspijeva da pokaže kako arhivski izvor obično sam po sebi ima neupitan autoritet u odnosu na gledaoca, ma koliko on bio iskrivljen, prerađen i pokrenut pomoću drugog sistema percepcije, kao i drugačijeg konteksta cirkulacije i pojavljivanja. Nasuprot tome, serija takođe nagovještava kako gledalac, i ovdje, može da povrati svoju kritičku poziciju ispred slike da bi iznova ispitao kako istorijski konstruisane percepcije djeluju na nas i na kraju oblikuju našu recepciju kada nam se predstave s narativom, objašnjenjem ili teorijom. Ni patos ni užas neće nas poštedjeti toga da sami odlučujemo.

Pornografska slika, kriminalna slika, arhivska slika: unutar svog sistema umjetnica prerađuje tri glavna registra savremene slike kako bi pažljivo stvorila uslove za krhku obustavu (ne)vjerovanja. Međutim, između ta tri režima slike postoji razlika koju treba utvrditi. Pornografska, kriminalna i arhivska slika takođe odgovaraju, u njihovoj preradi od strane umjetnice, određenoj tehnomedijskoj paradigmi unutar koje cirkulišu. Naime, arhivska slika takođe iziskuje da se čita u okviru trenutne sklonosti da se apstrakcija doživljava kao tržište istine, dok se transparentnost, naprotiv, sada stavlja pod sumnju da postaje opresivna. Jedan od najočiglednijih primjera te promjene najbolje se može primijetiti u umjetničkoj paradigmi koja je bila široko rasprostranjena početkom minule decenije, a koja na kraju prenosi vjeru u emancipatorsku prirodu nevidljivosti i suštinske vrijednosti toga „da se nešto ne vidi".[16] I drugi su, možda na manje pojednostavljen način, ukazivali na apstrakciju svojstvenu mašinskom vidu, sistemima nadzora i obrascima za ekstrakciju podataka[17] ili su formulisali „konkretnu i uzročnu vezu između složenosti sistema s kojima se svakodnevno susrijećemo; neprozirnost s kojom je većina tih sistema konstruisana ili opisana; i temeljnim, globalnim pitanjima nejednakosti, nasilja, populizma i fundamentalizma".[18]

SA ONE STRANE ISTINE, DOKAZA, IDENTIFIKACIJE I PROVJERE ČINJENICA

Kao subjekti mejnstrim medijske kulture 21. vijeka suočavamo se s potrebom da se odučimo od slijepog povjerenja u sliku kao dokaz i počnemo da se udaljavamo od priređene vrijednos-

15   Za slike: Darja Bajagić, *The Murder of the Sign*; *Frustum — Numero 11: Komadat Logora Mamula (Piece of Mamula Camp)* or *Komandat Logora Mamula (Commander of Mamula Camp*; *Threshold (Gigantomachy Con- cerning a Void)*; *Gateway to the Gulf*; *The Ambivalence of the Sacred*, sve 2024. Za skulpturu: Darja Bajagić, *Limb Immobilizer (Iron Rings to Which Some Prisoners Were Tied)*, 2024.

16   Tema ustajanja protiv i podrivanja prepoznavanja lica ponavlja se u radovima i knjigama iz 2010-ih kod umjetnika kao što su Hito Stajerl ili Zak Blas.

17   Vidi, na primjer, radove Trevora Paglena.

18   Džejms Brajdl, *Novo mračno doba*, London. Verso Books, 2018, str. 12.

ti istine koju smo skloni da bespogovorno pripisujemo istorijskom dokumentu. Treba samo uzeti u obzir širenje izrazito slikovitih prizora rata u vijestima na društvenim mrežama, taj jezivi prostor gdje se samokomodifikacija stapa sa opštom apstrakcijom stvarnog, gdje se sve vrste predstava spajaju i miješaju u poplavi slika bez porijekla, slika nevezanih ni za kakve stvarne koordinate, to jest, sada potpuno generisanih slika vještačke inteligencije. To takođe podrazumijeva da predstava koja je odveć grafička, odveć precizna ili odveć detaljna odmah postaje sumnjiva: upravo je ta vrsta slika, ranije skrivena (*istinita jer je skrivena*), sada postala sumnjiva (*sumnjiva jer je izložena*). Bajagić i dalje ne zanima da otkriva bilo kakvu istinu, niti gaji vjeru u njeno ikonografsko postojanje; umjesto toga, ona nas, posmatrače, uporno tjera da se suočavamo sa sivom zonom, gdje ćemo, naposljetku, iznova i iznova, morati sami da odlučujemo, ili riješiti, ali tek nakon što se budemo odučili, da uopšte ne odlučujemo.

Sadašnje vrijeme nam daje zadatak da preispitamo istinitost vrijednosti arhiva, ali to inherentno pripisivanje vrijednosti ni ovdje se nigdje ne može bolje vidjeti no kao kroz slijepu vjeru svijeta umjetnosti u to.[19] Početkom 21. vijeka kvazireligijska vjera u sliku kao dokaz sija svjetlije nego ikada, a to se posebno vidi u arhivskom dokumentu, u nizu praksi koje su se sada okrenule traženju suštinske istine u molekularnim, atomskim porama stvarnosti. Za neke od onih umjetnika tragalaca vrijednost istine se ponovo razbuktala: ona je tu, ali jednostavno ne možemo da je vidimo, što znači da bi nas usavršavanje novih tehnoloških oruđa dovelo do krajnjeg otkrivanja. Pitanje mehaničke vizije i njenog odnosa prema stvarnosti nije novo. Valter Benjamin je već suprotstavio dva konceptualna lika: mađioničara i hirurga, što je odgovaralo slikaru i snimatelju. On smatra da potonji „prodire duboko u tkivo predmeta"[20] i, iz predigitalnog vizuelnog okruženja, već radi s djelovima i preradama, mijenja trajanje vremena, prostora i tačke gledišta. Veza koja se može pronaći s našim sadašnjim vremenom nije izričita, ali se ipak može vidjeti da označava početak naše trenutne algoritamski osmišljene proizvodnje sadržaja: porijeklo sada tražimo u nevidljivim porama stvarnosti. Dakle, vrijednost istine nije napuštena, već je proširena potraga za njom.

Istina, dokaz, identifikacija, provjera činjenica;[21] tehnike prepoznavanja slika, javno dostupne alatke za prikupljanje informacija, kulturna analitika:[22] to su aktuelne paradigme 2020-ih uz koje i prema kojim se novi rad Darje Bajagić mora čitati. Opus radova o Mamuli, predstavljen na 60. Međunarodnoj izložbi umjetnosti – La Biennale di Venezia, ukazuje na unapređenje ikonografskih režima koji čine cjelinu njenog rada dodavanjem trećeg, arhivskog sloja, na dva već postojeća, pokazujući kako njen umjetnički sistem može da obuhvati promjenljivu prirodu medijske cirkulacije i sistema vjerovanja posmatrača-učesnika. Ovdje, dok novo medijsko okruženje teče uporedo s napredovanjem samih umjetnika, ikonološki izvori, estetske strategije i politike posmatranja Bajagić takođe se mogu pročitati u tome kako se taj sistem razlikuje u odnosu na taj niz praksi i njihovo podrazumijevano uokvirivanje stvarnosti. U Imperiji, ili njenom metonimijskom pristupu opusu, ne postoji više zajednica, a samim tim ni interpretativna zajednica na koju bismo se mogli osvrnuti. U neoliberalnom globalnom svjetskom poretku, vječito hladnom, uvijek uglađenom i nadasve atomizovanom u svom individualističkom društvenom rasporedu, participativno posmatranje i dalje može postojati kao vodeće načelo, ali se u isto vrijeme mora preformulisati kao radikalno jedinstven poduhvat: odavno su nestale grupne predrasude iz kojih su ideologija ili religija crple svoj mir i utjehu. Neoliberalni limb samo povećava težinu perceptivne slobode koju nam Darja Bajagić ovdje pruža: to je sloboda, ali ne liči na oslobođenje, sa dvije oštrice i teška za udove kao okov za gležanj. Iz takvog čina ikonografskog i semiotičkog odučavanja možemo dobiti ono što će nas ostaviti na mukama slobode i suočiti sa egzistencijalnim strahom od izbora. Kada bismo, međutim, odlučili da učestvujemo u igri, sasvim svjesni šta prihvatanjem težine preuzimamo; ako prihvatimo da uđemo u predstavu i provedemo vrijeme u tom suspendovanom prostoru senzorne rekonfiguracije, mogli bismo biti oslobođeni trajne privlačnosti lažnih algoritamskih izvjesnosti. Čovjeku je stvarno potrebno ostrvo.

19   Temeljnu analizu dotične pojave daje Kler Bišop u svom članku „Preopterećenost informacijama", *Artforum*, 61 (80), april 2023.

20   Benjamin, *Op. cit.*, XIV.

21   Za slike vidi, na primjer, forenzičku arhitekturu uopšte; za zvuk Lorensa Abu Hamdana uopšte.

22   Lev Manovič, *Kulturalna analitika*, 2020.

ARTWORKS
RADOVI

*Frustum — Numero 11: Komadat Logora
Mamula (Piece of Mamula Camp) or
Komandat Logora Mamula (Commander
of Mamula Camp)*

2024

Acrylic and UV print on canvas; steel frame
Akril i UV print na platnu; čelični okvir

246 × 274 × 4 cm

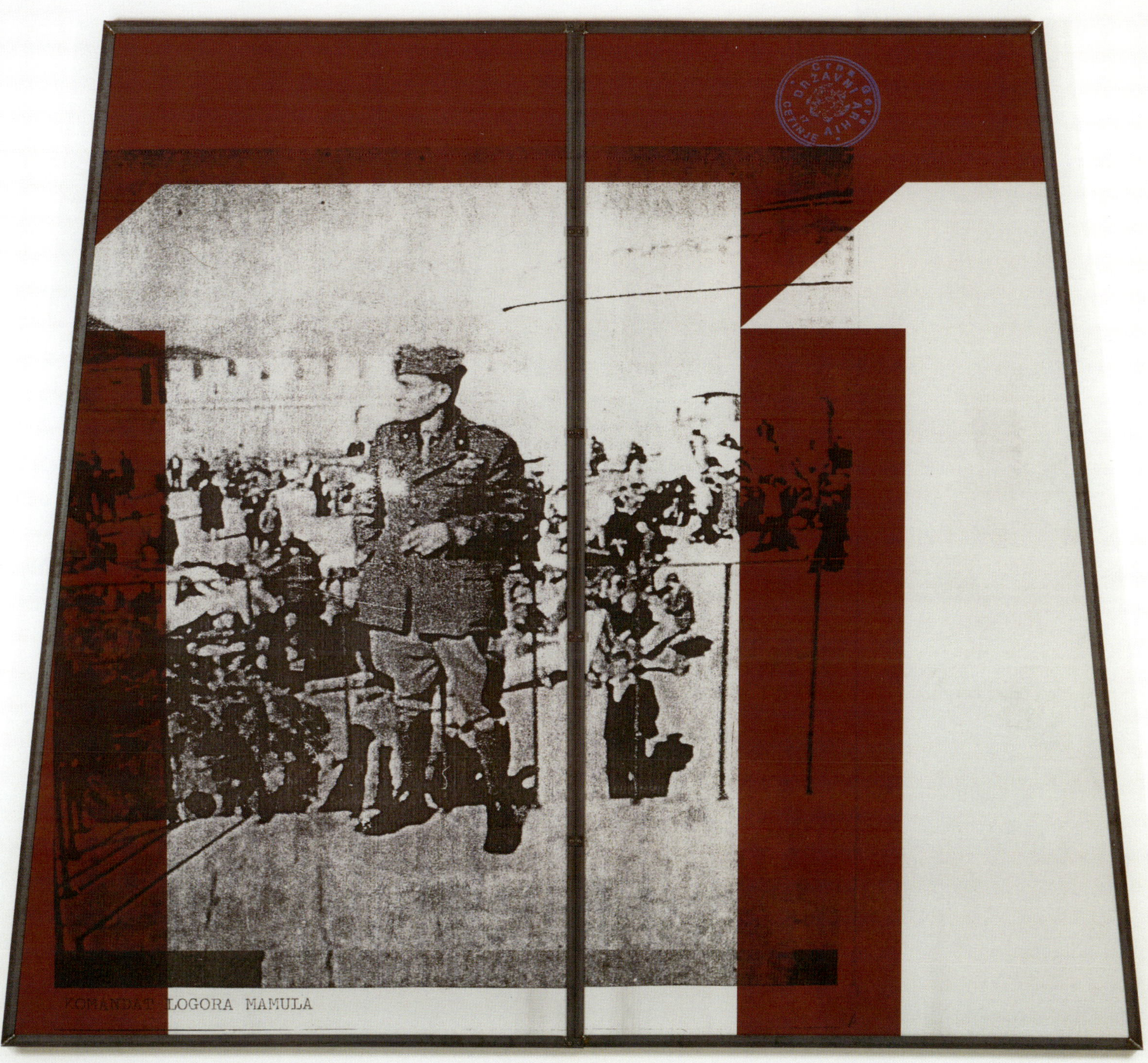
KOMANDAT LOGORA MAMULA

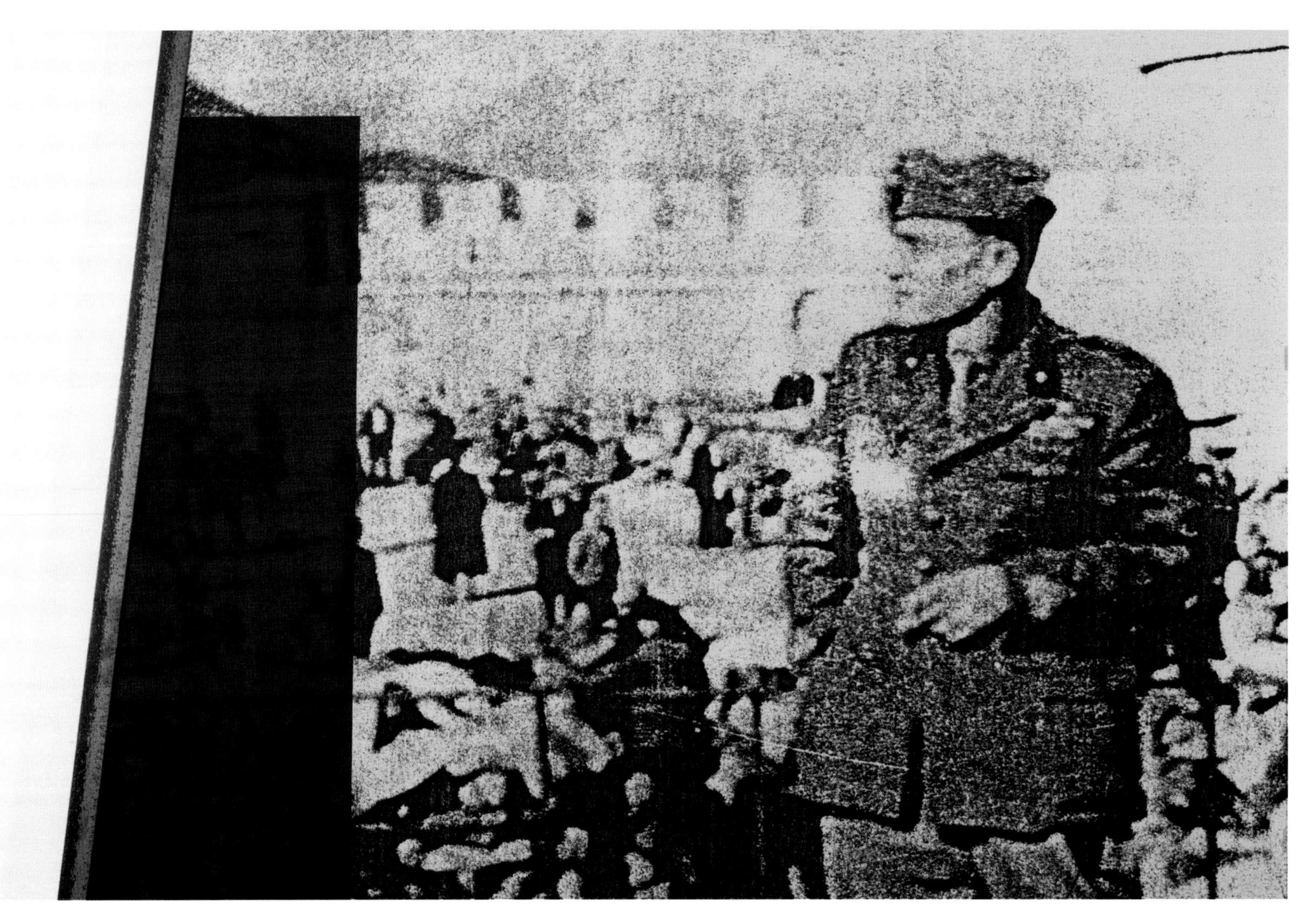

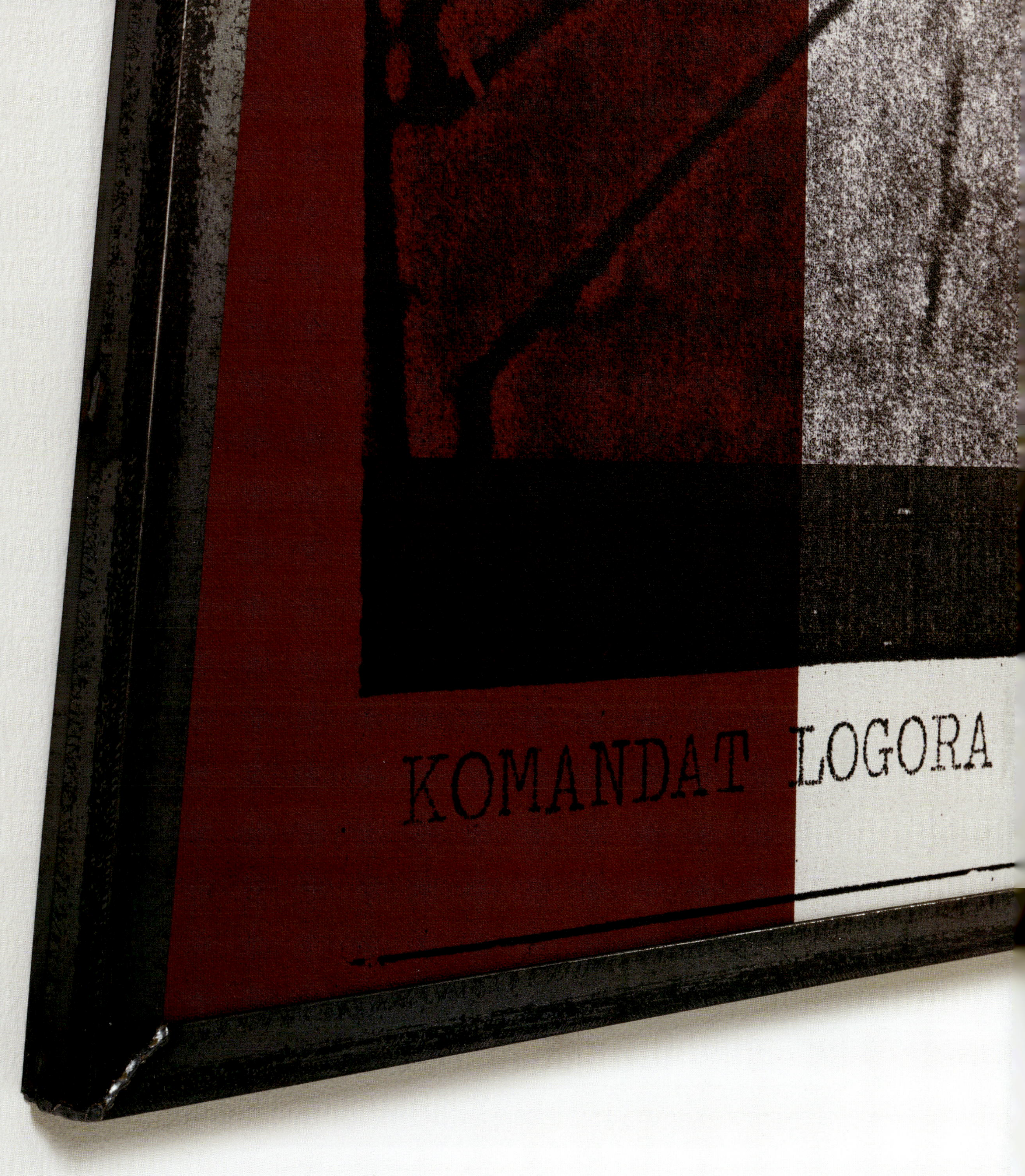

KOMANDAT LOGORA

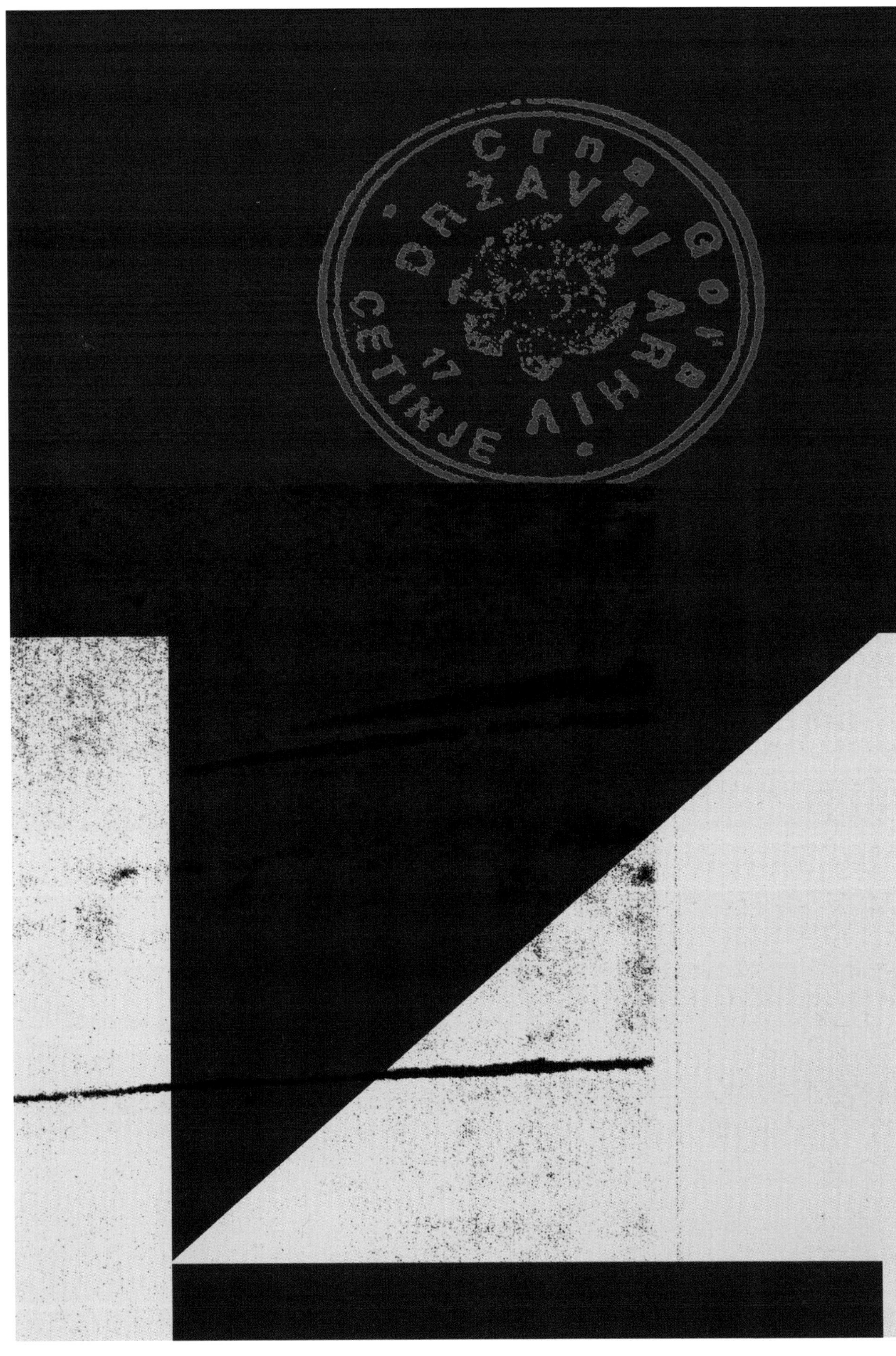

Crna Gora
DRŽAVNI ARHIV
CETINJE
17

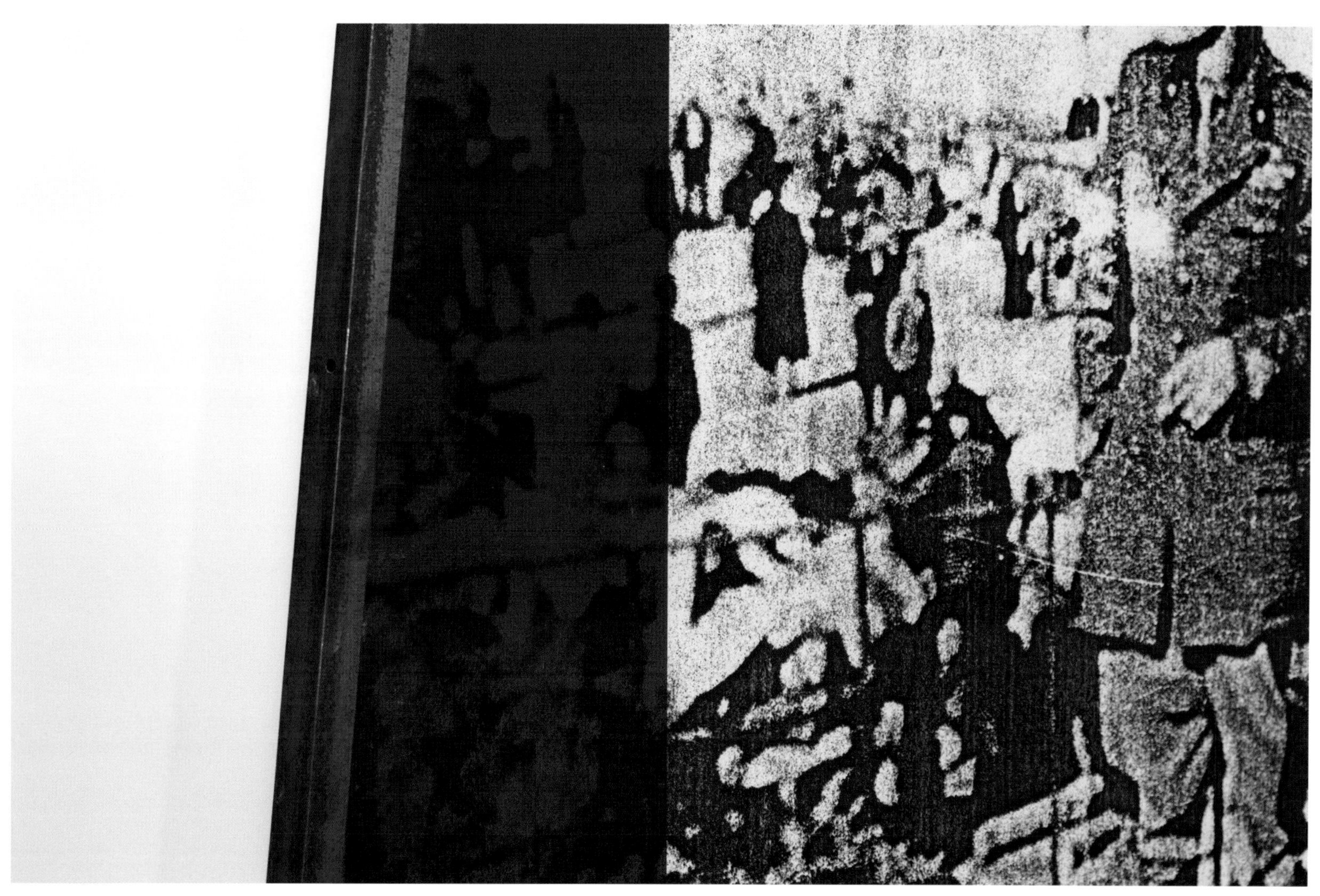

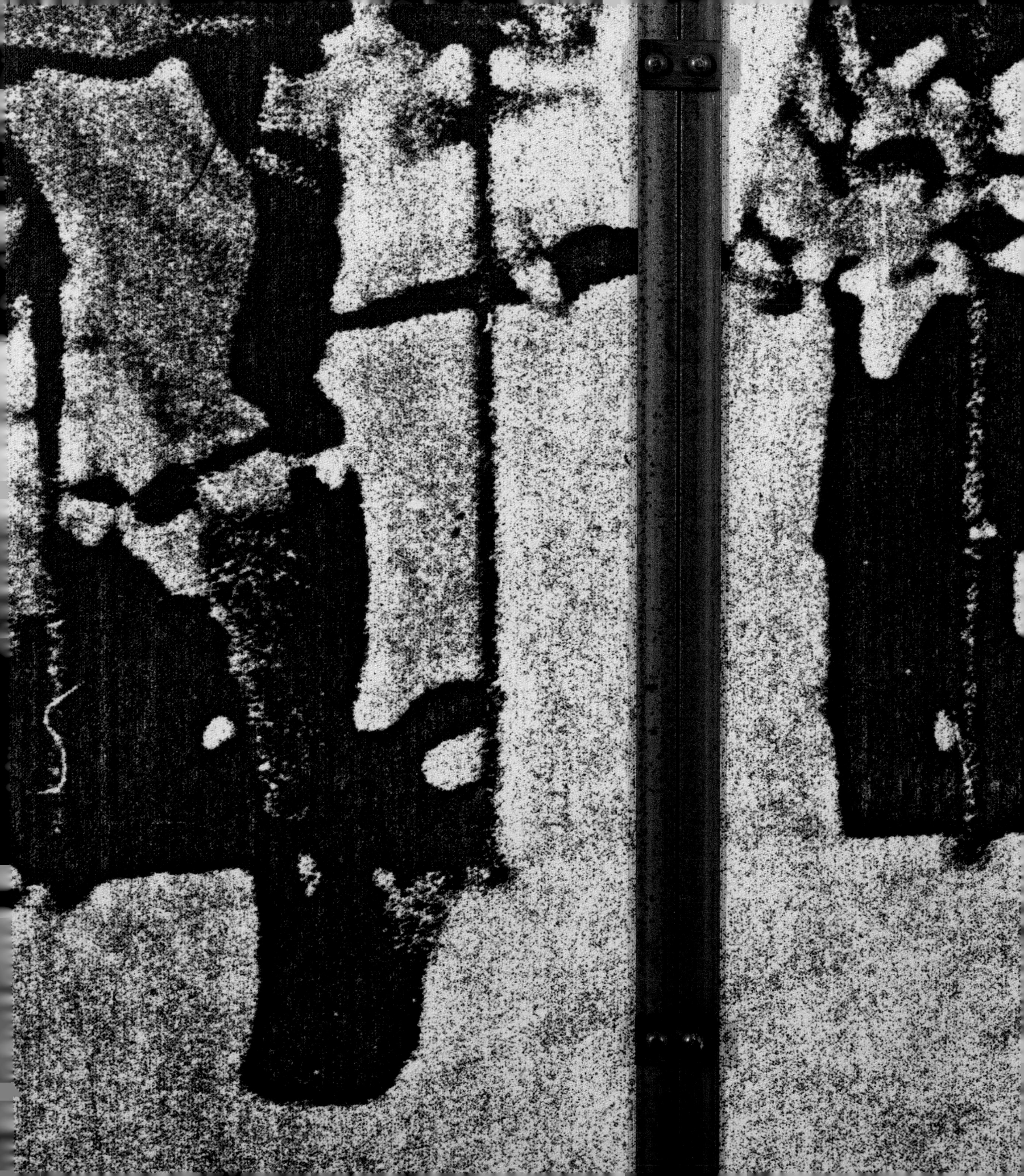

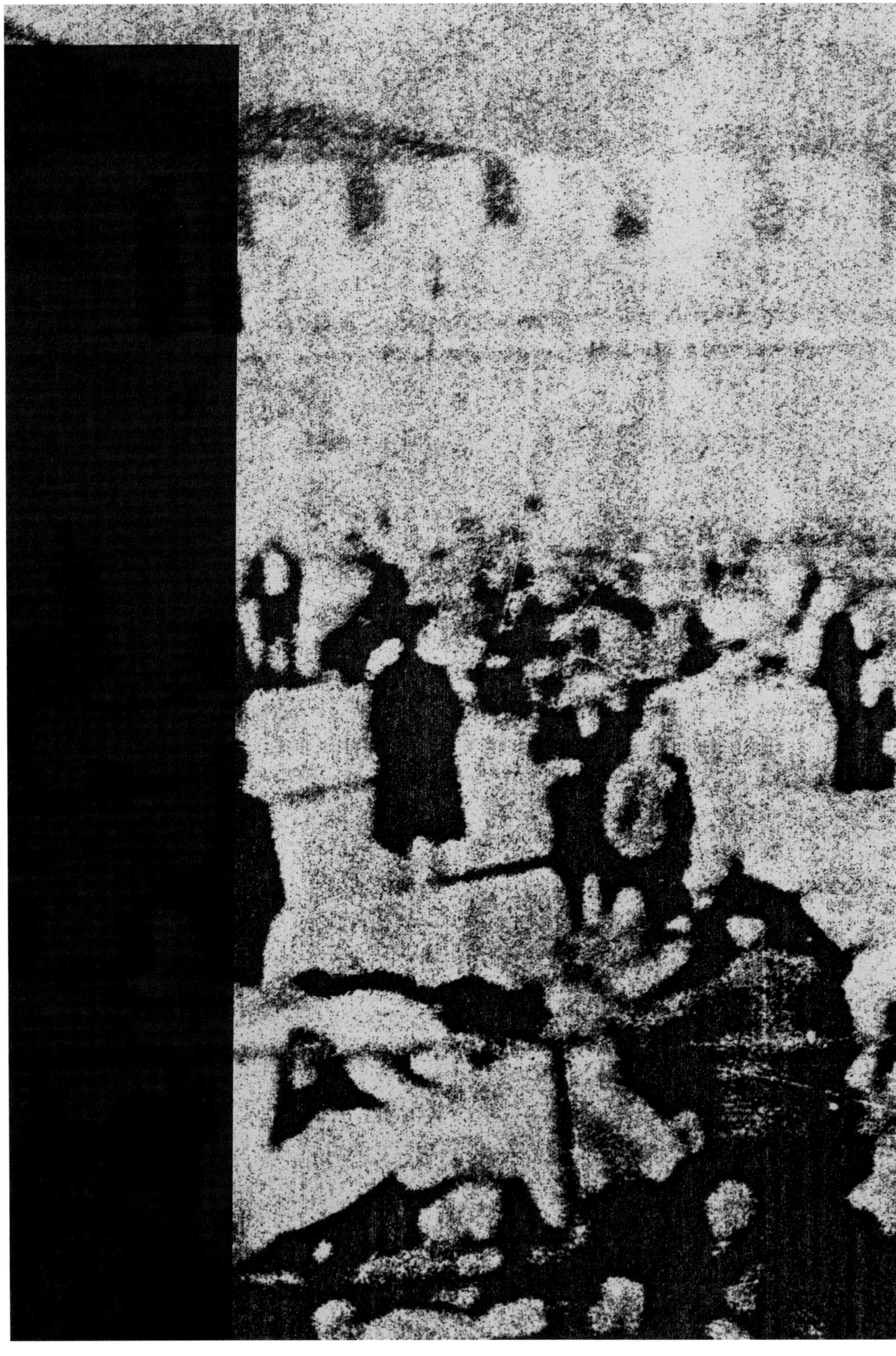

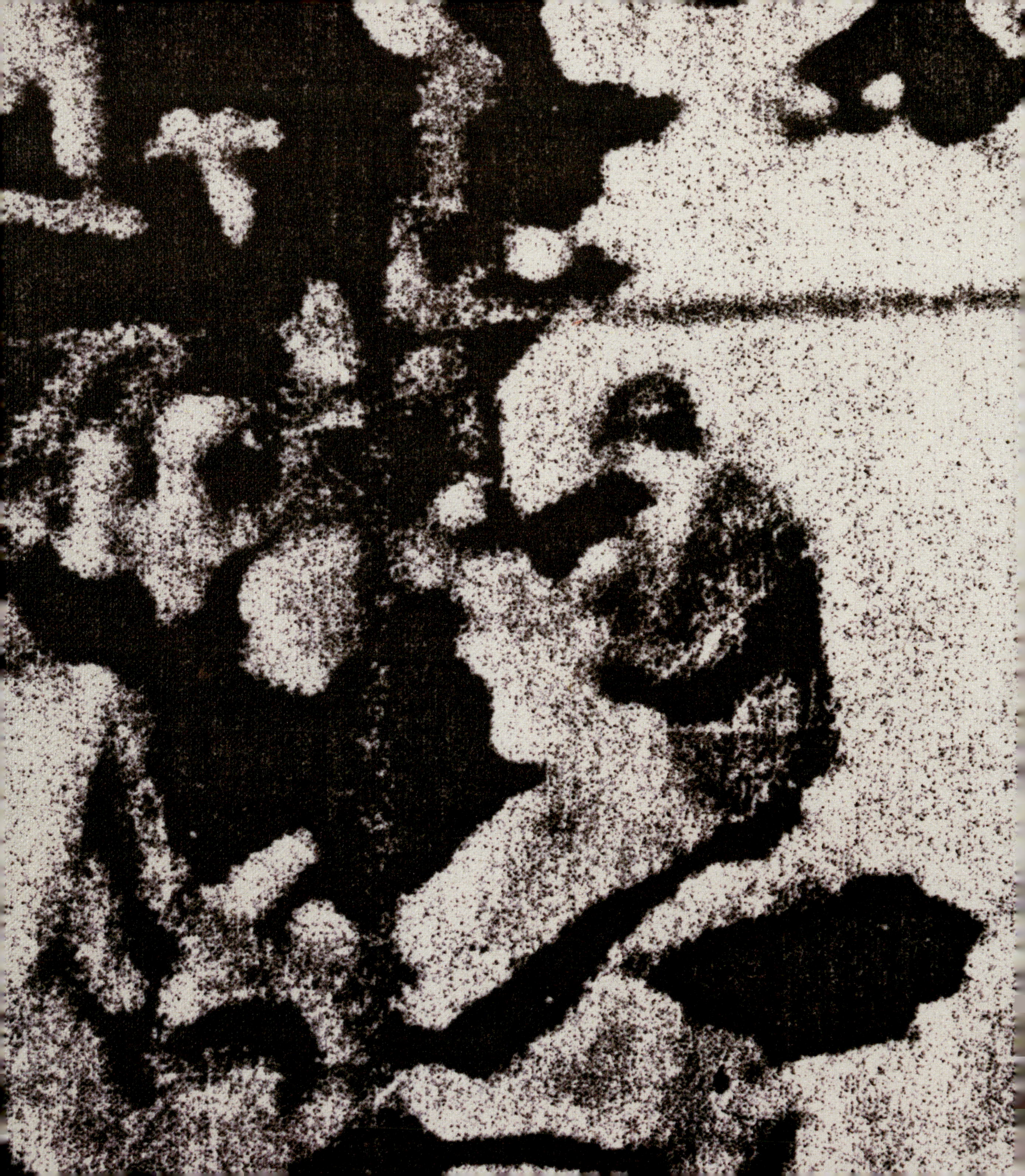

2024

Acrylic on military camouflage print fabric; steel frame
Akril na vojnom kamuflažnom platnu; čelični okvir

172 × 128 × 4 cm

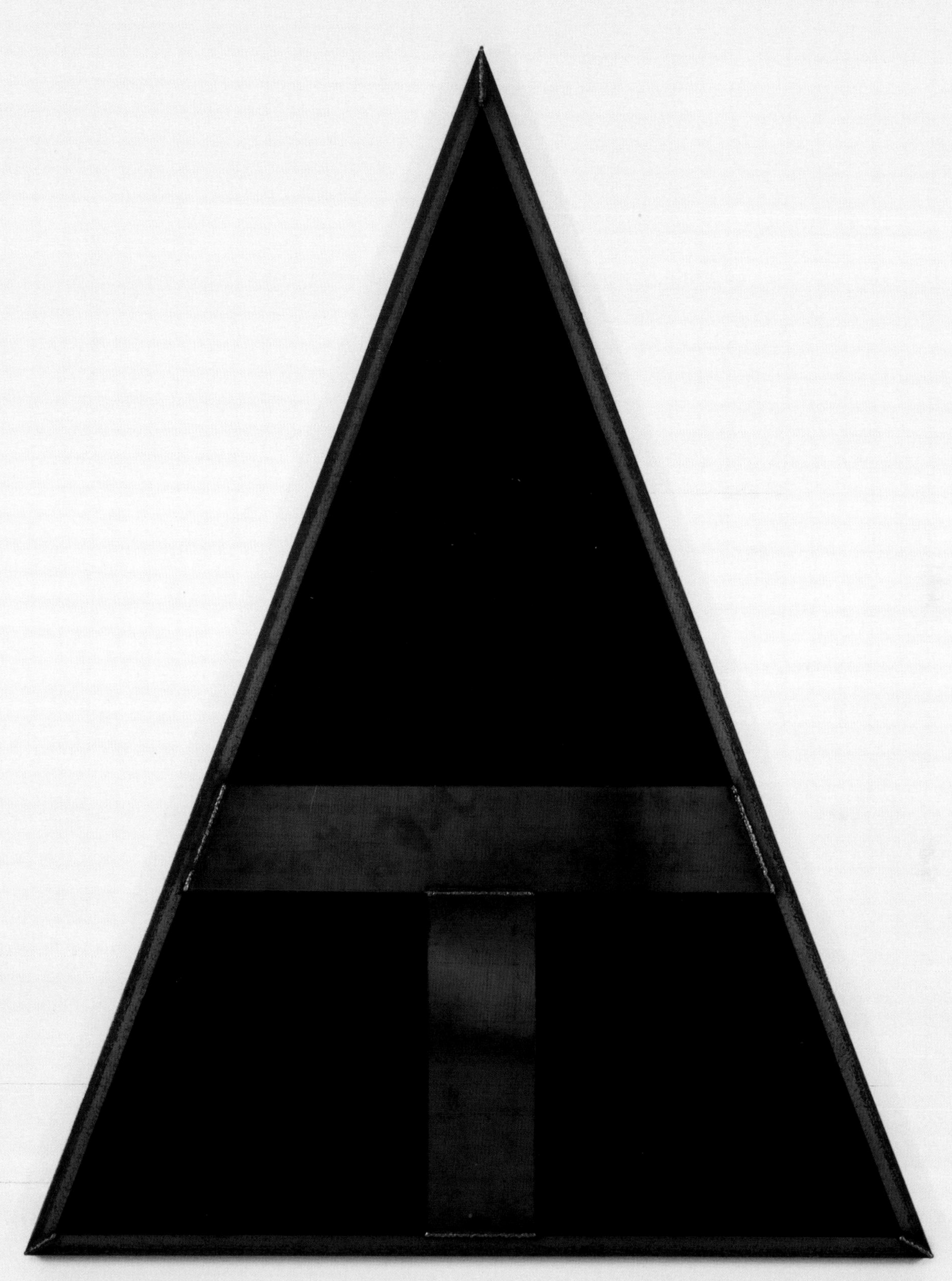

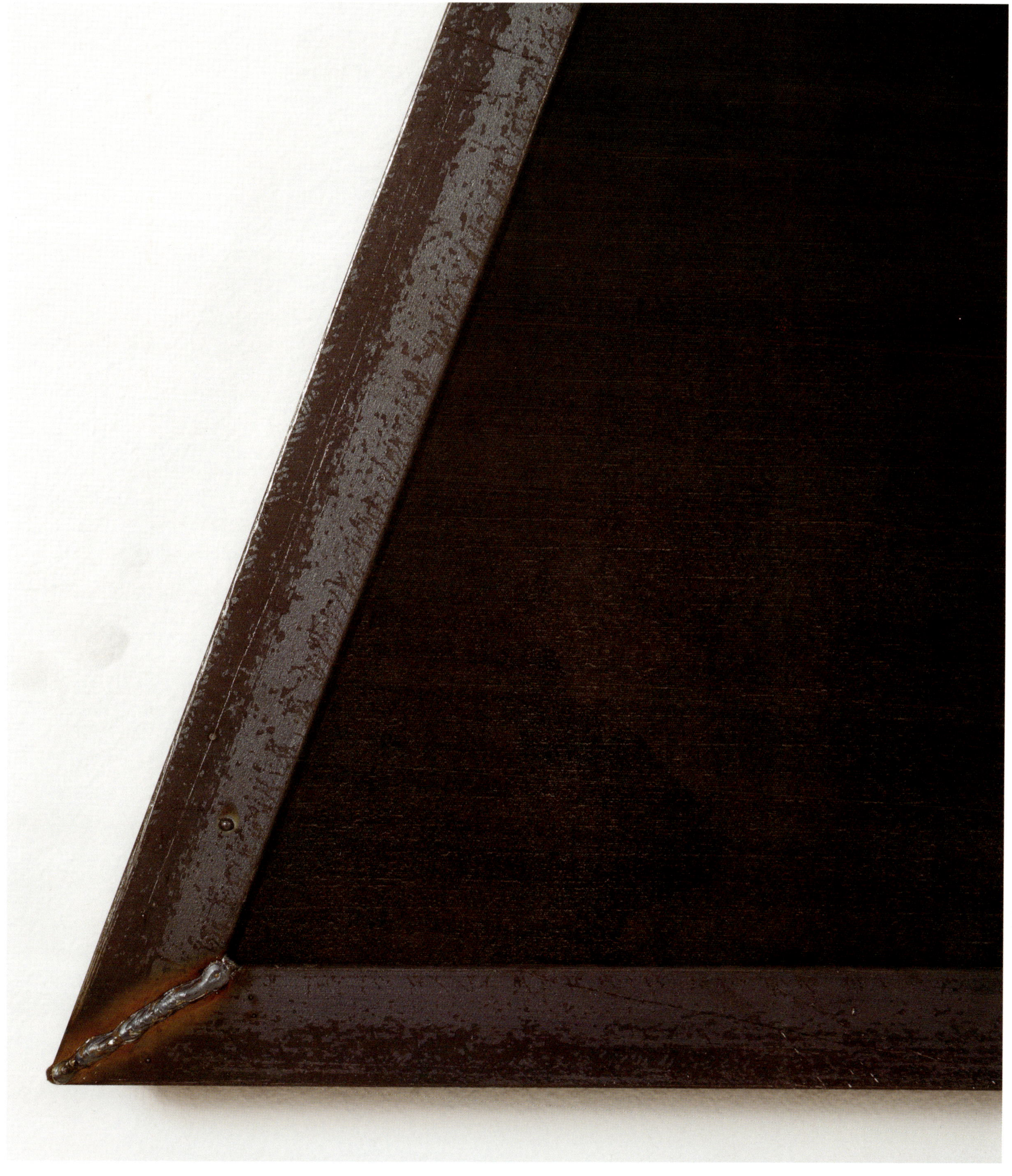

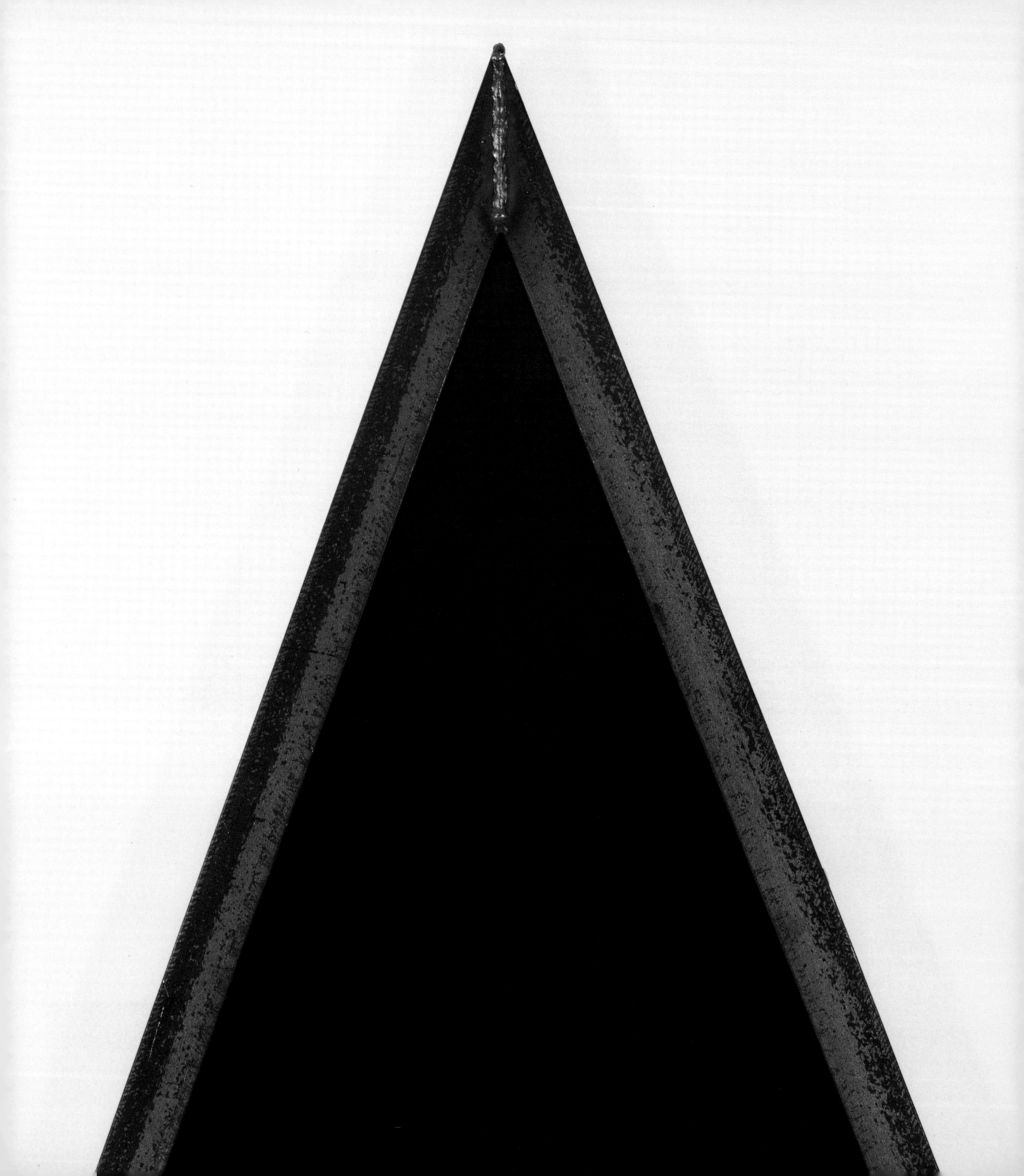

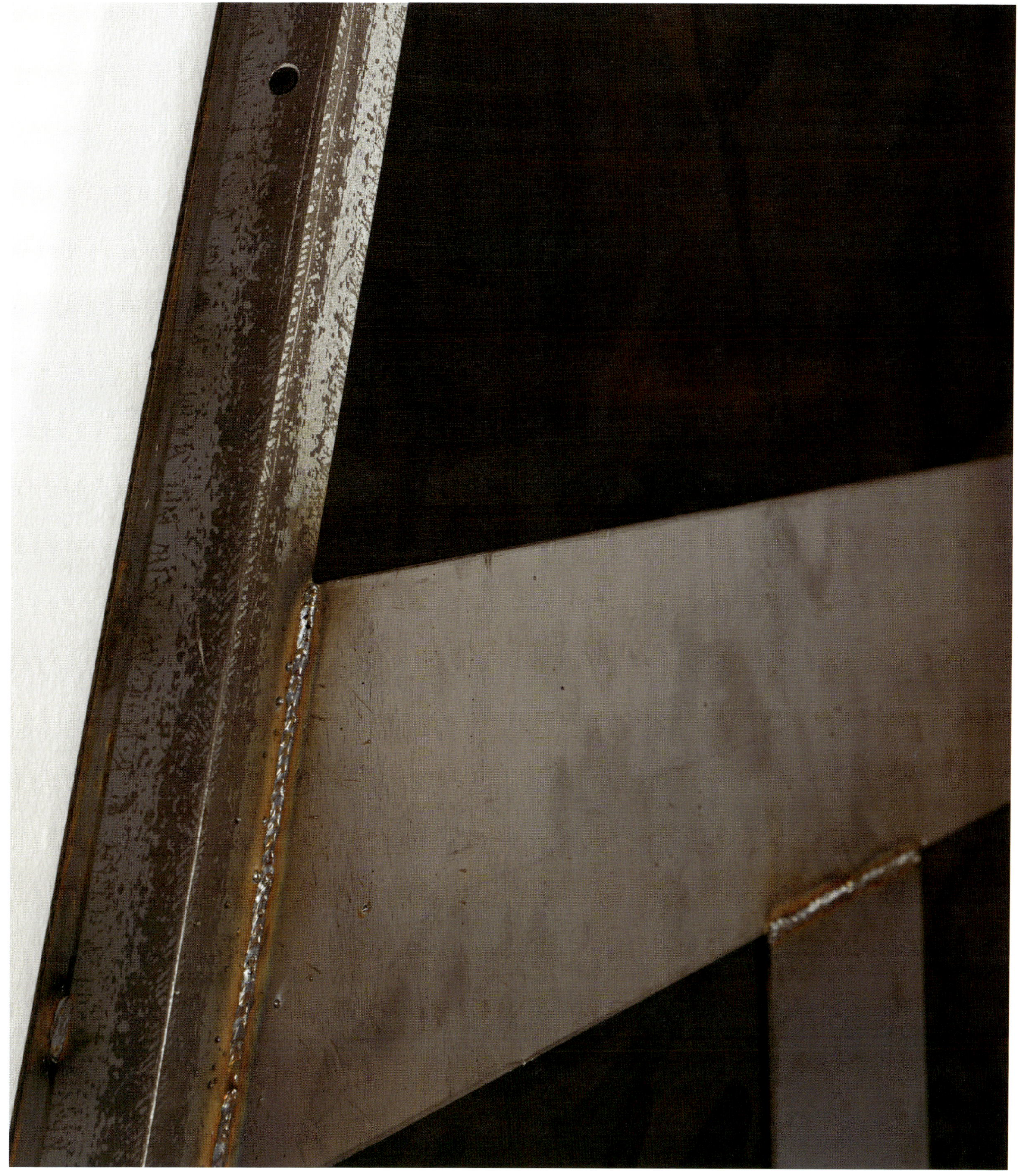

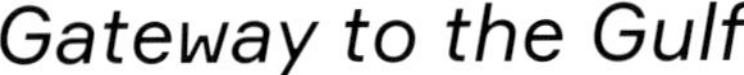

Gateway to the Gulf

2024

Acrylic and UV print on canvas; steel frame
Akril i UV print na platnu; čelični okvir

197 × 129 × 4 cm

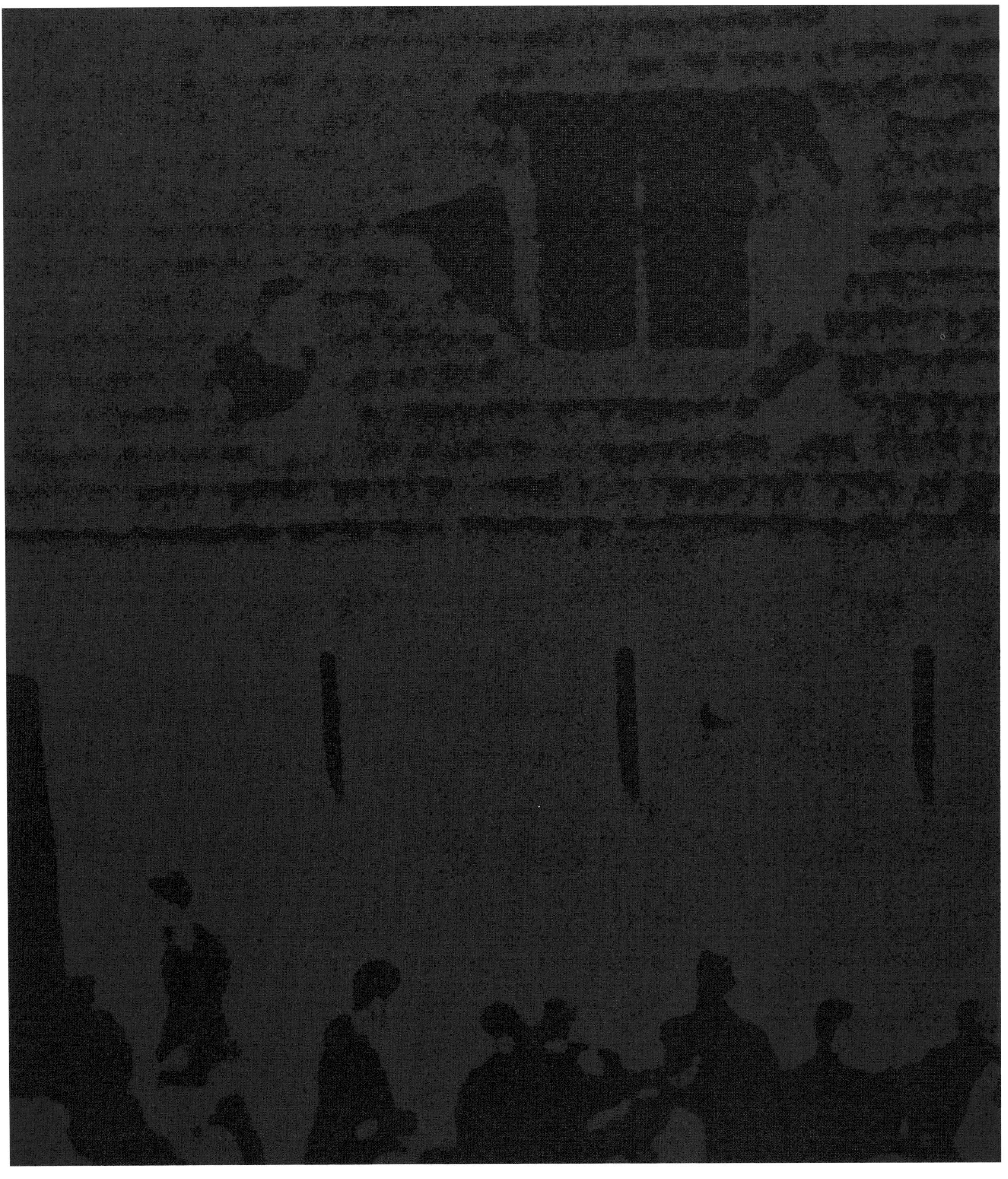

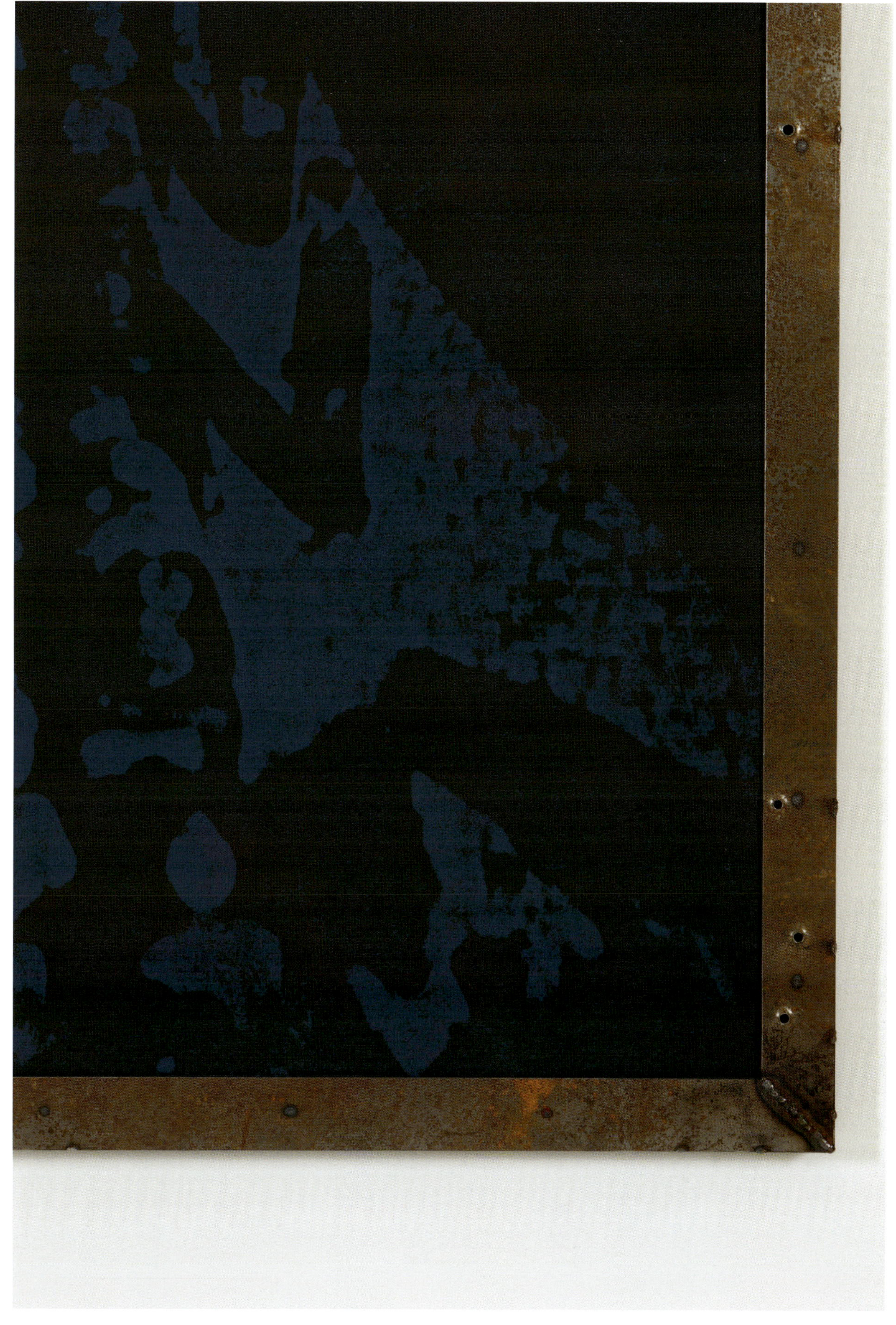

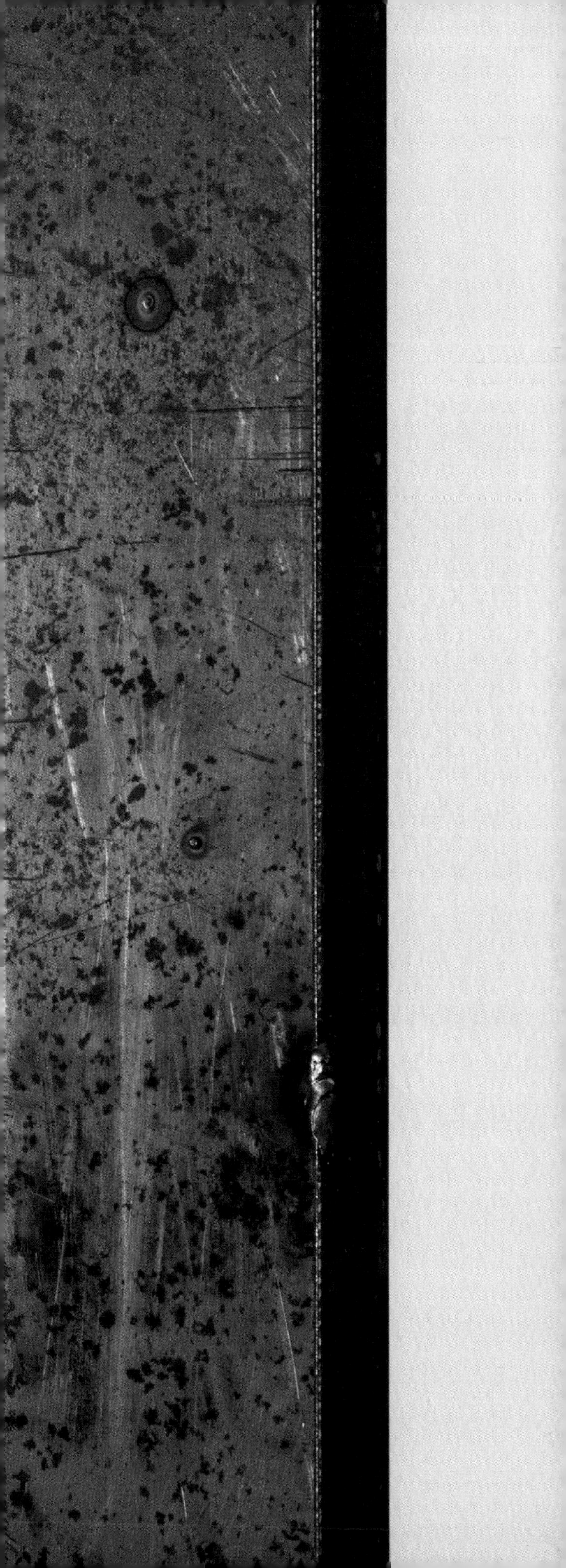

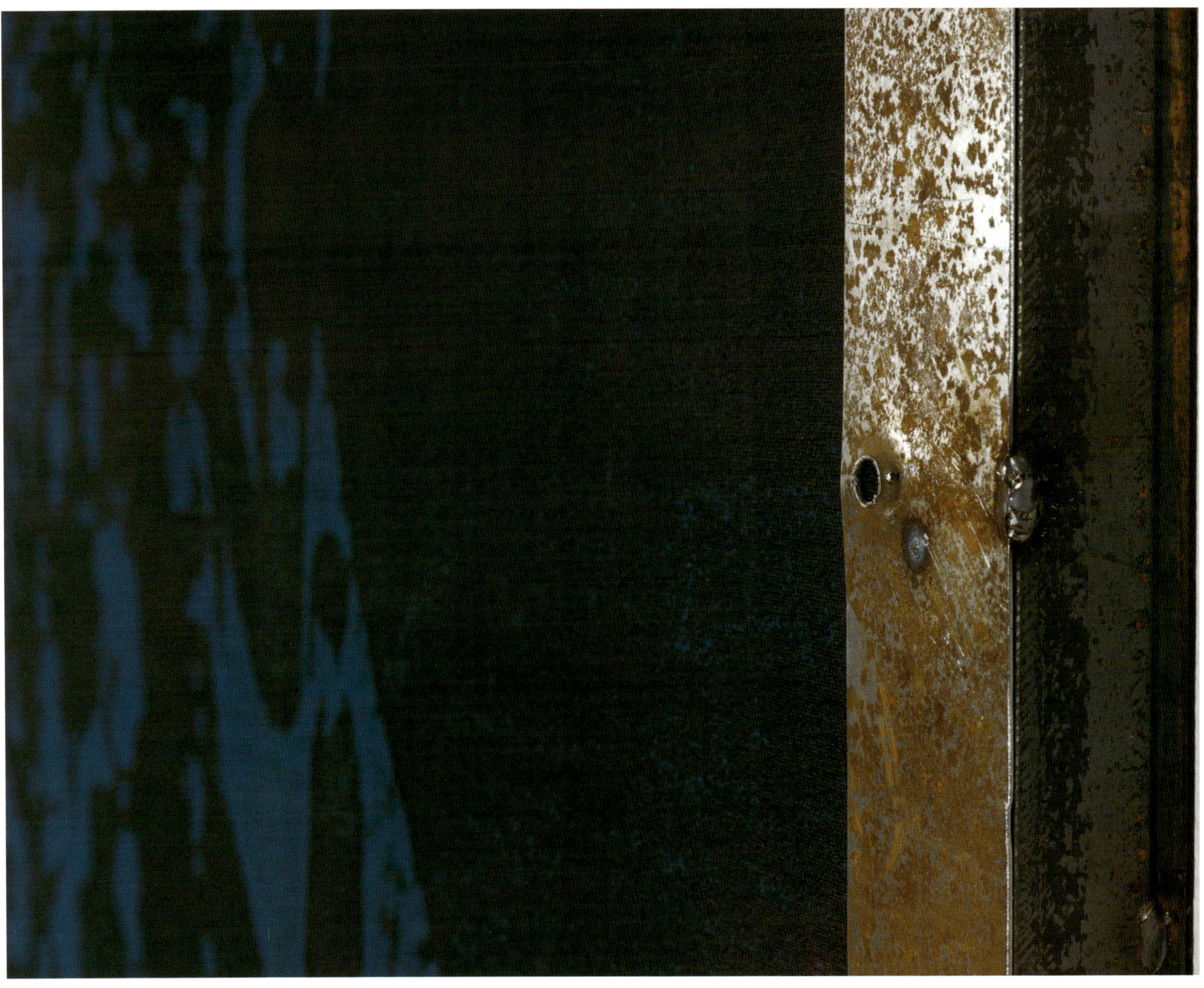

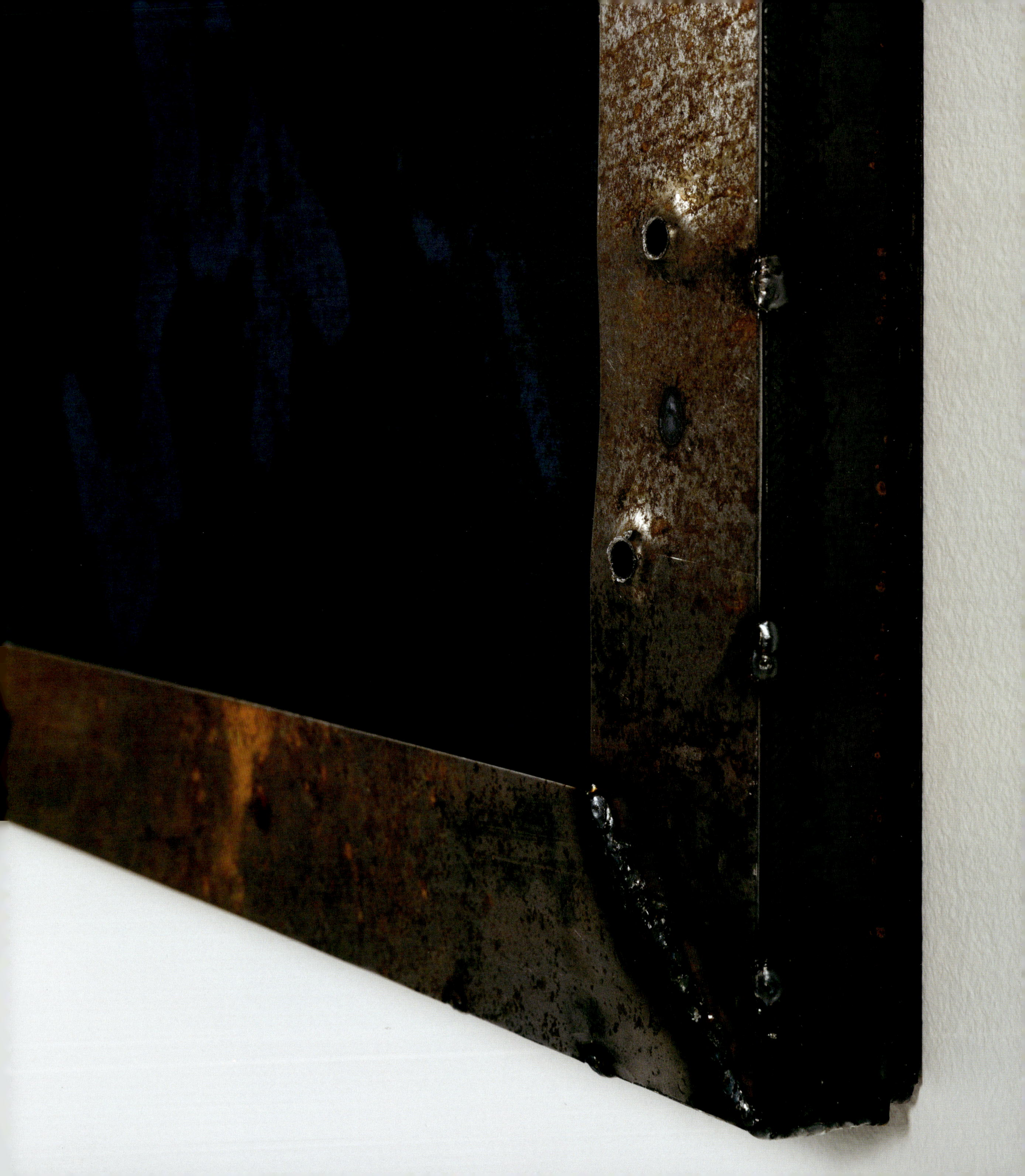

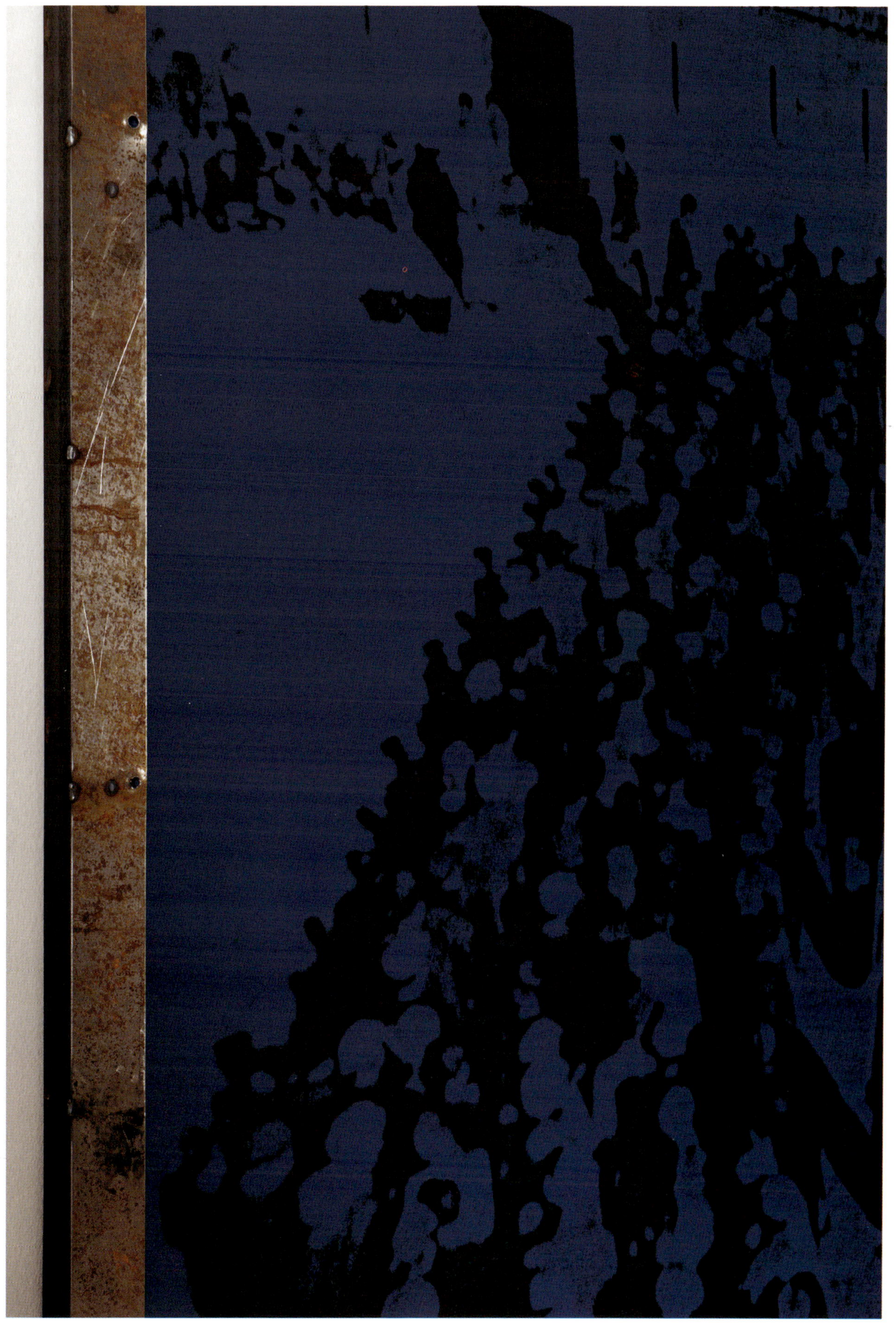

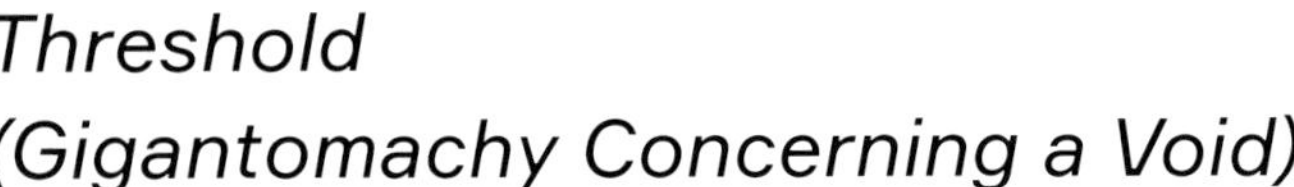

Threshold
(Gigantomachy Concerning a Void)

2024

Acrylic, canvas, concrete pigment powder, dirt, enamel paint, and UV print; steel frame
Akril, platno, betonski pigment u prahu, zemlja, farba, i UV print; čelični okvir

274 × 137 × 4 cm

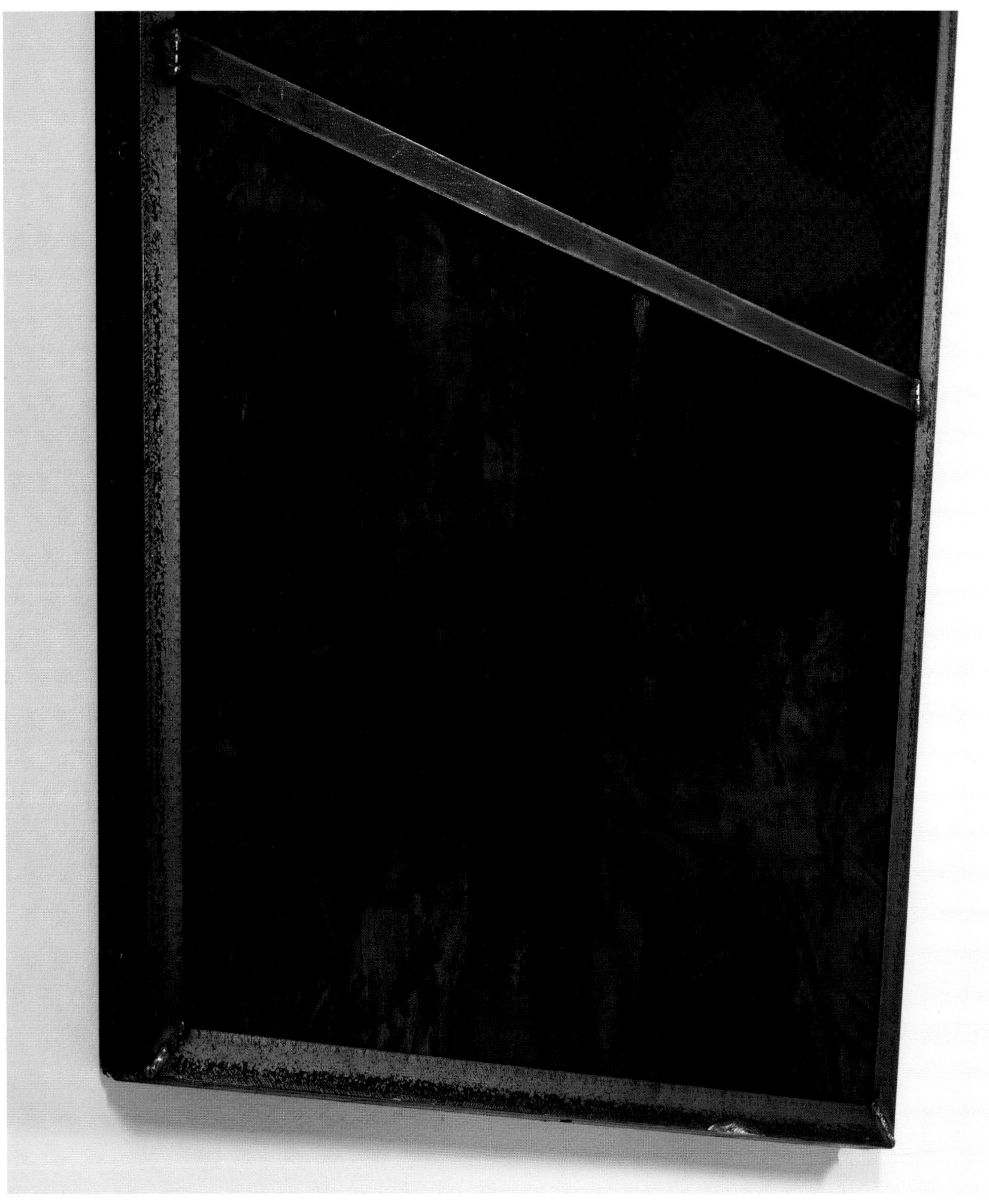

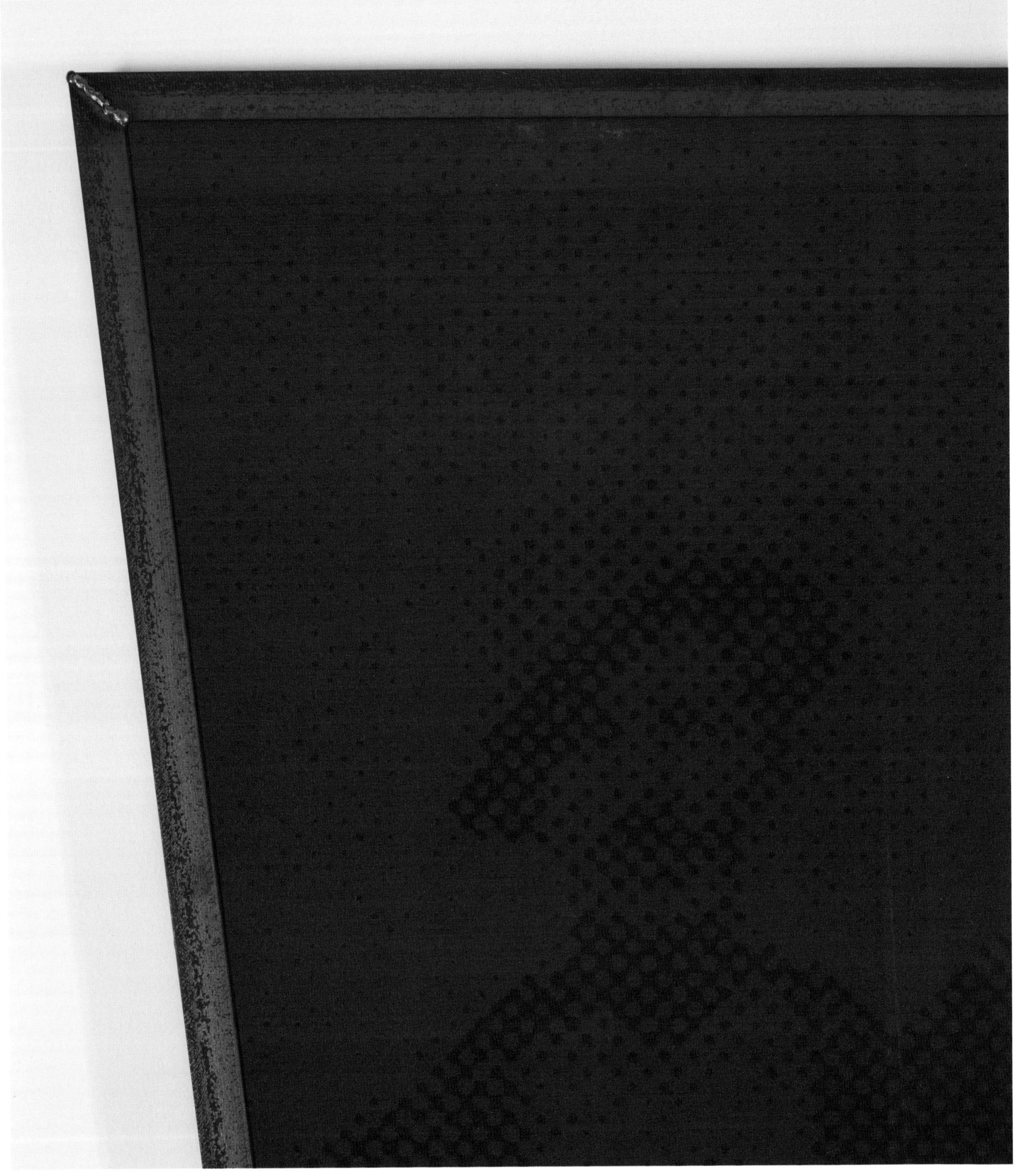

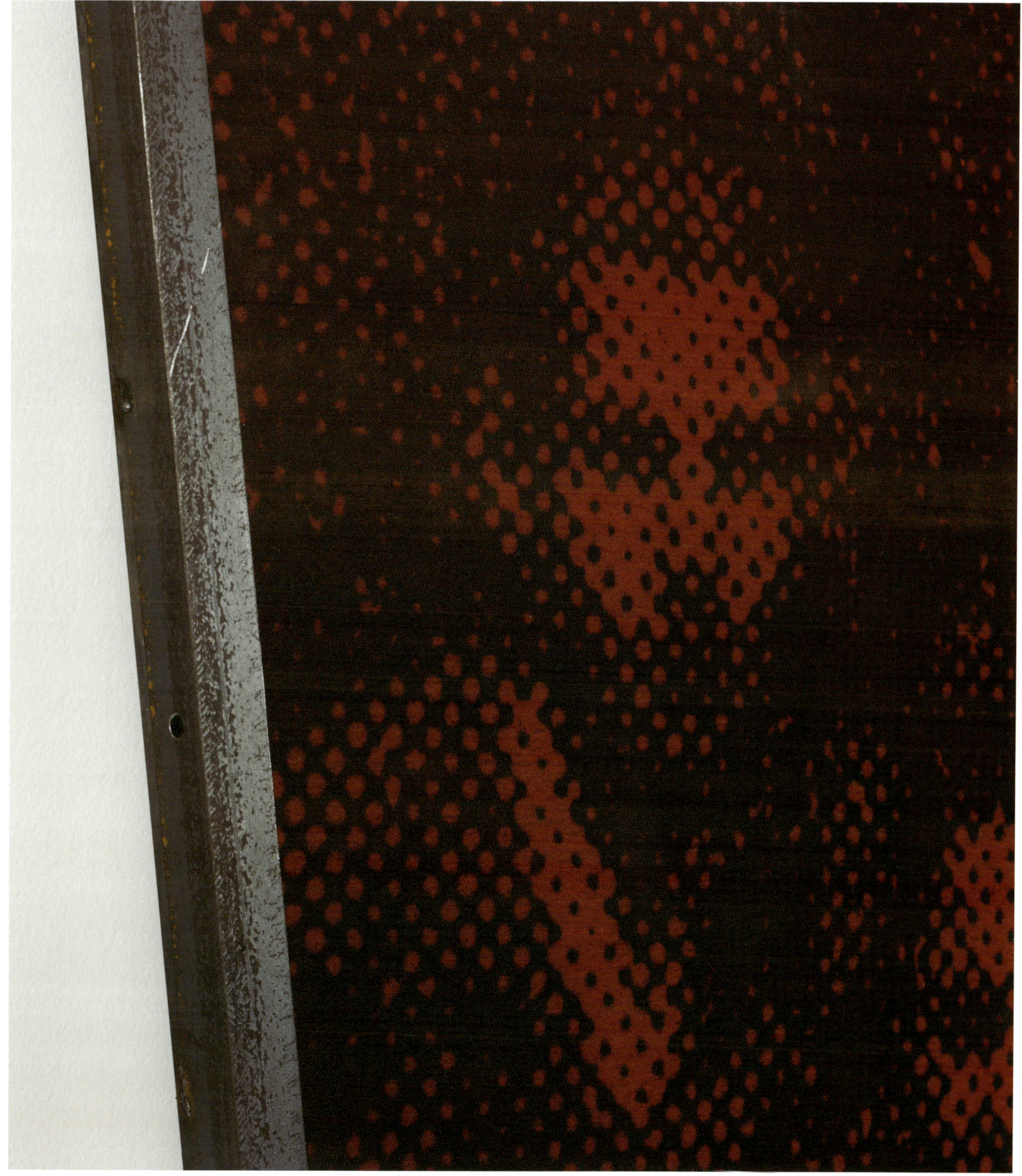

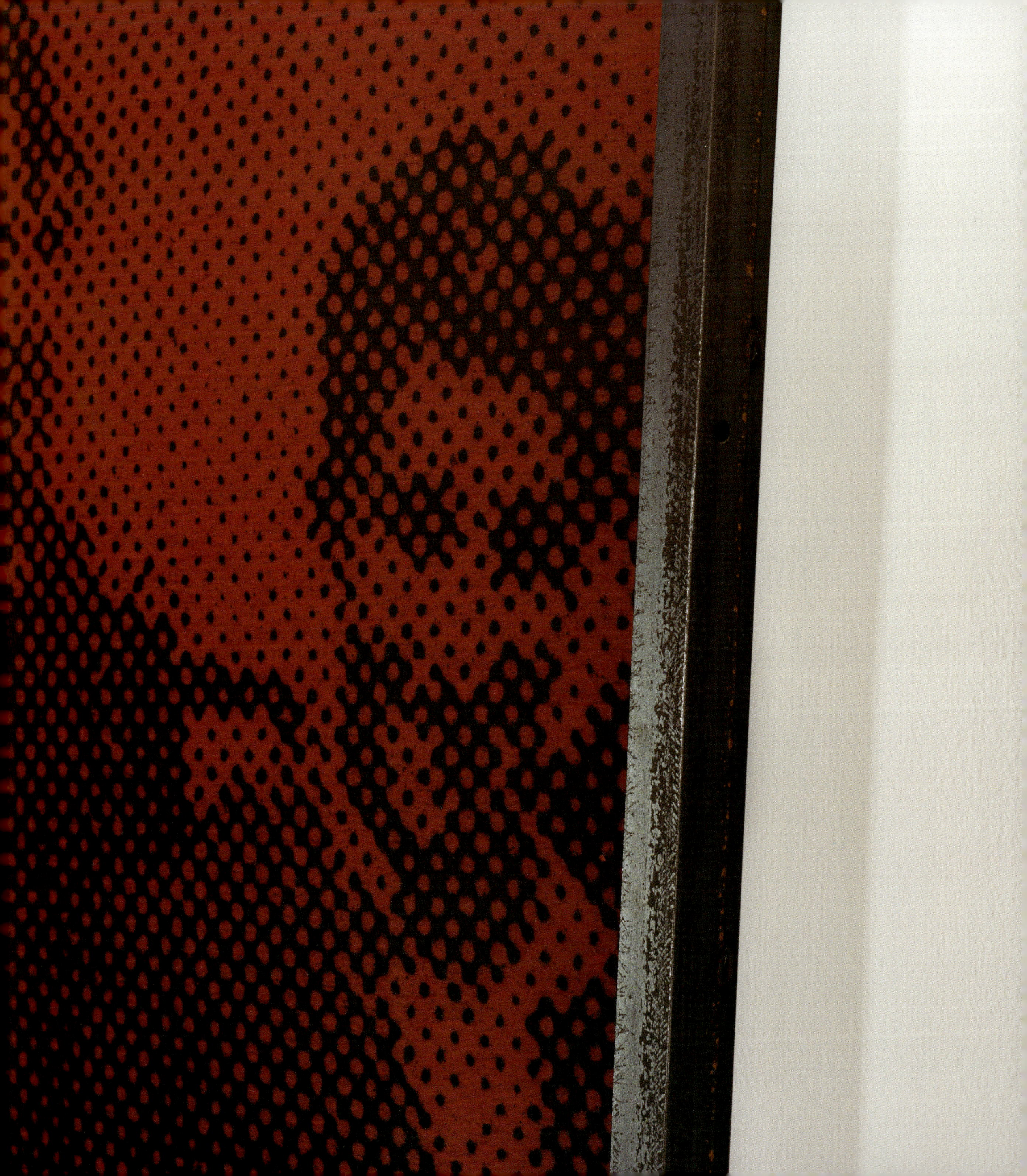

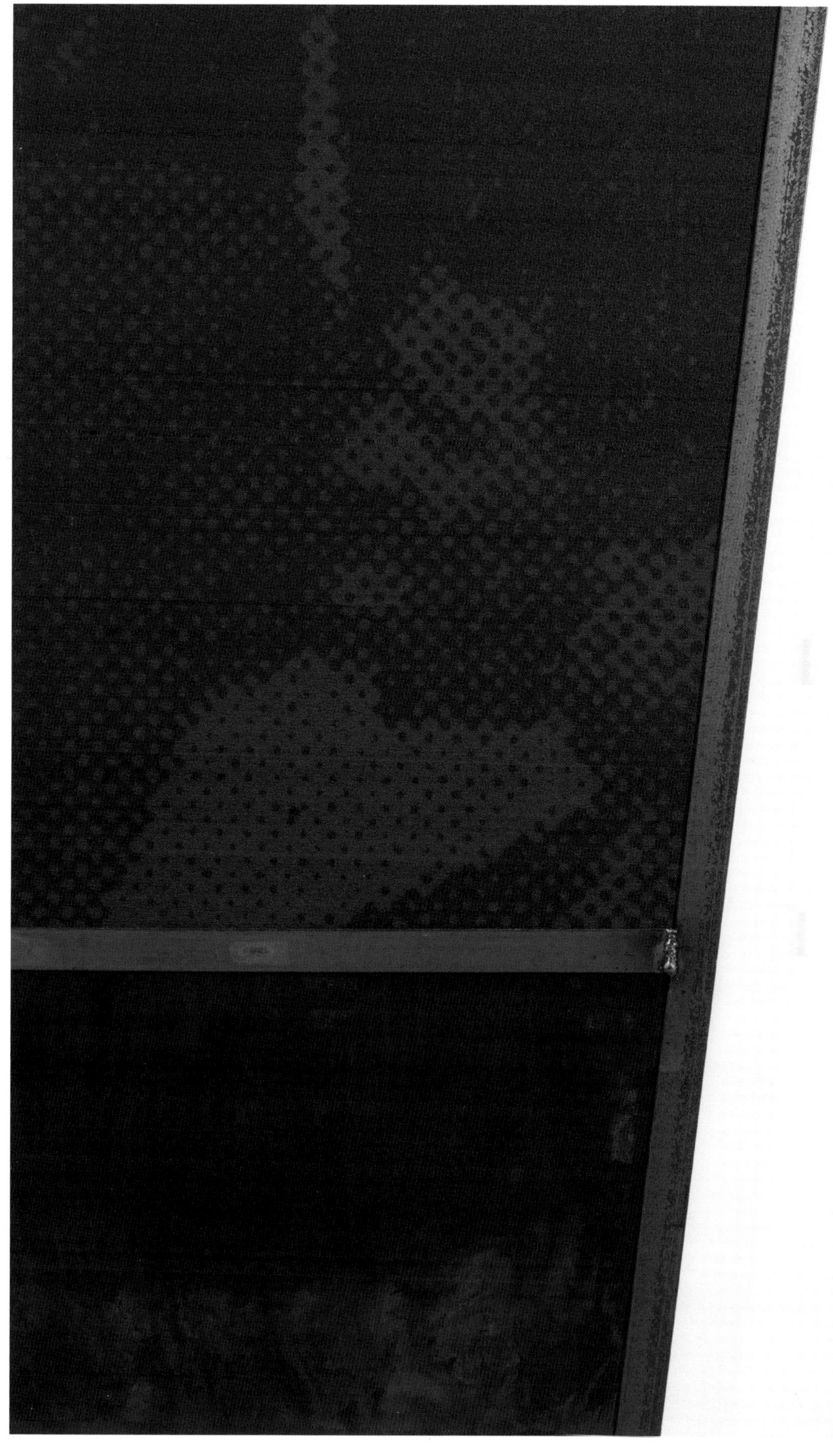

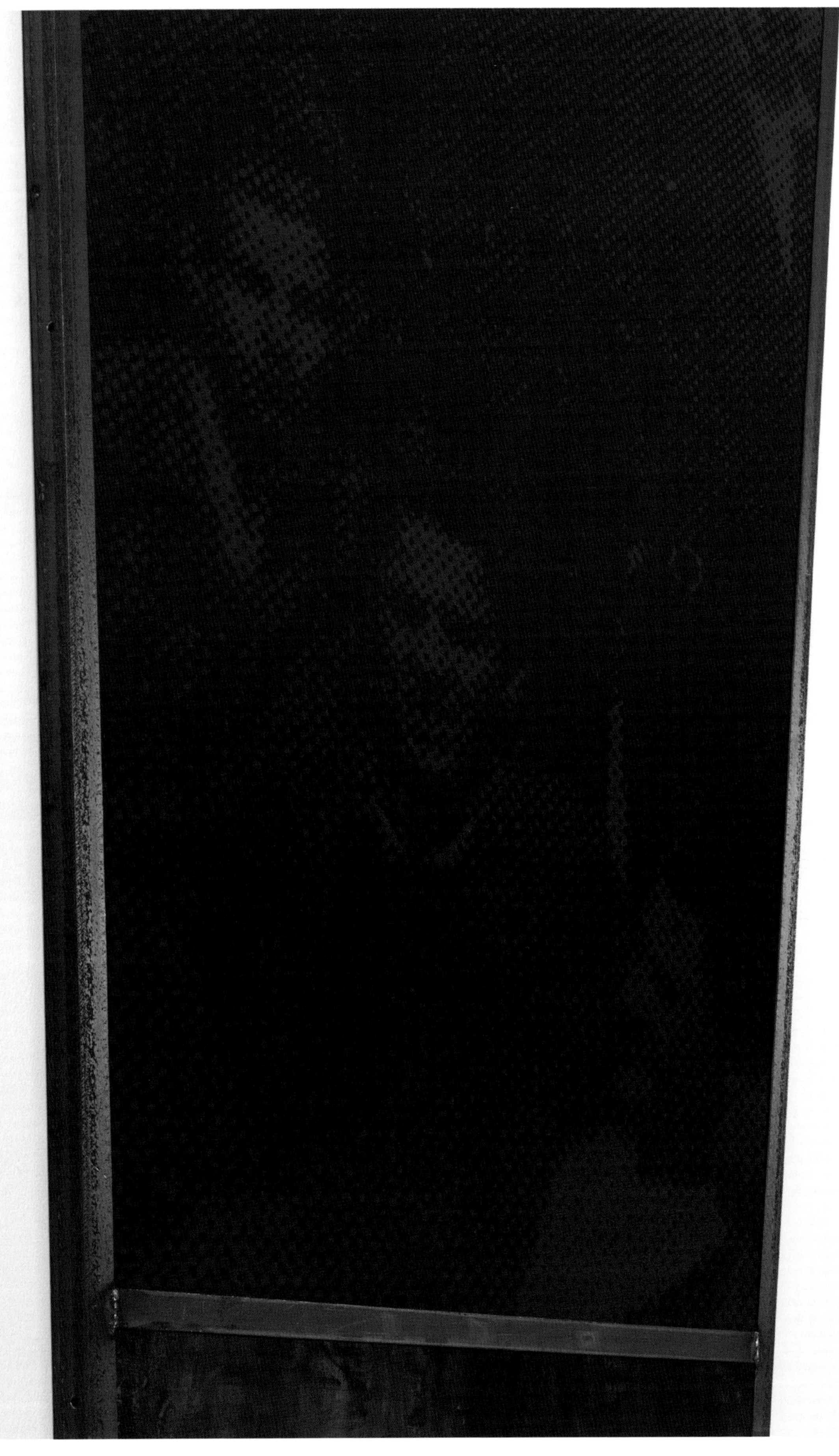

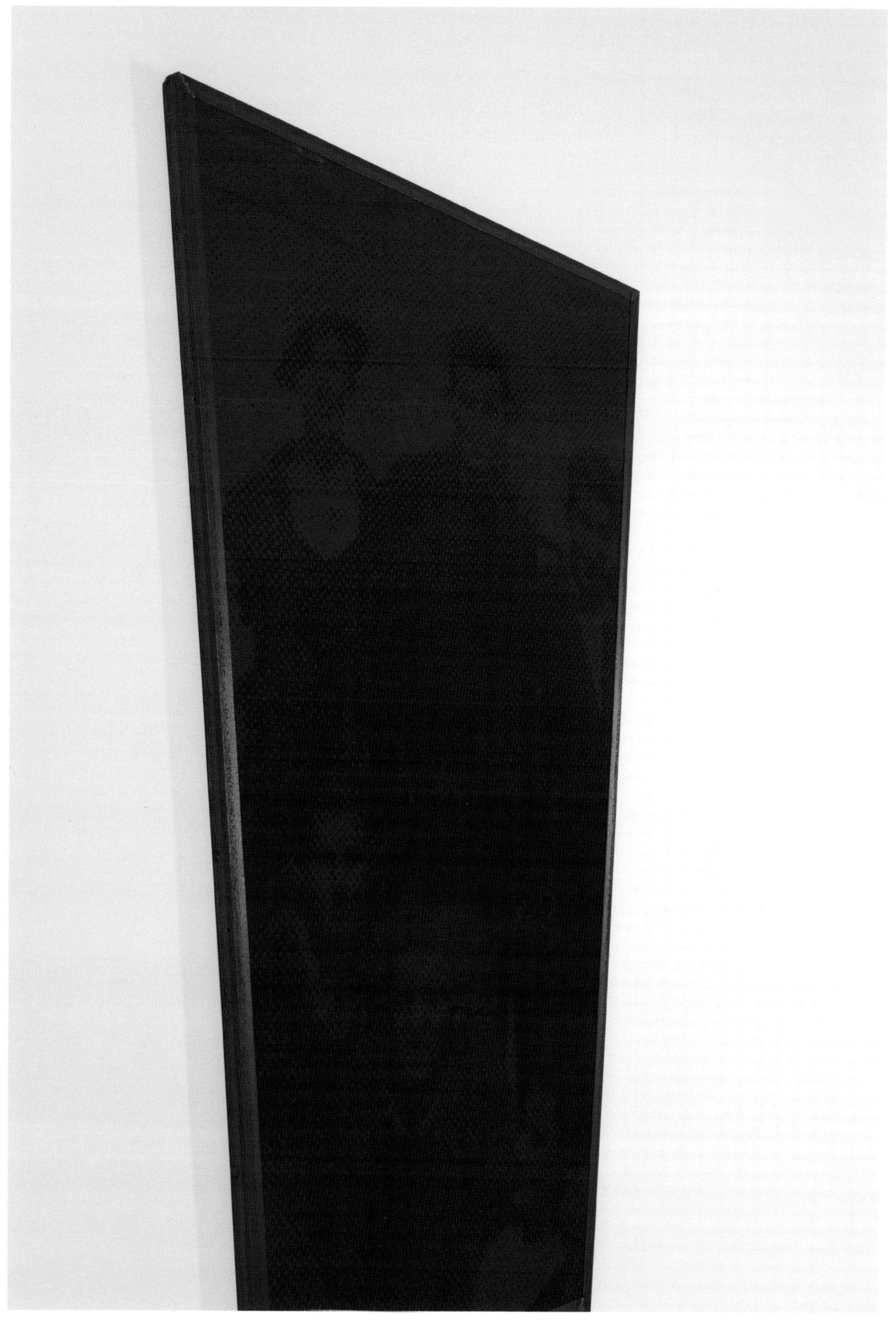

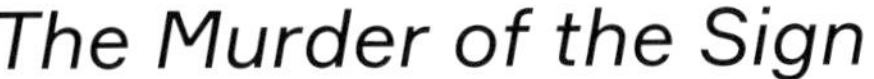

The Murder of the Sign

2024

Acrylic, canvas, defective military camouflage print fabric, dirt, and UV print; steel frame
Akril, platno, oštećeno vojno kamuflažno platno, zemlja, i UV print; čelični okvir

202 × 231 × 6 cm

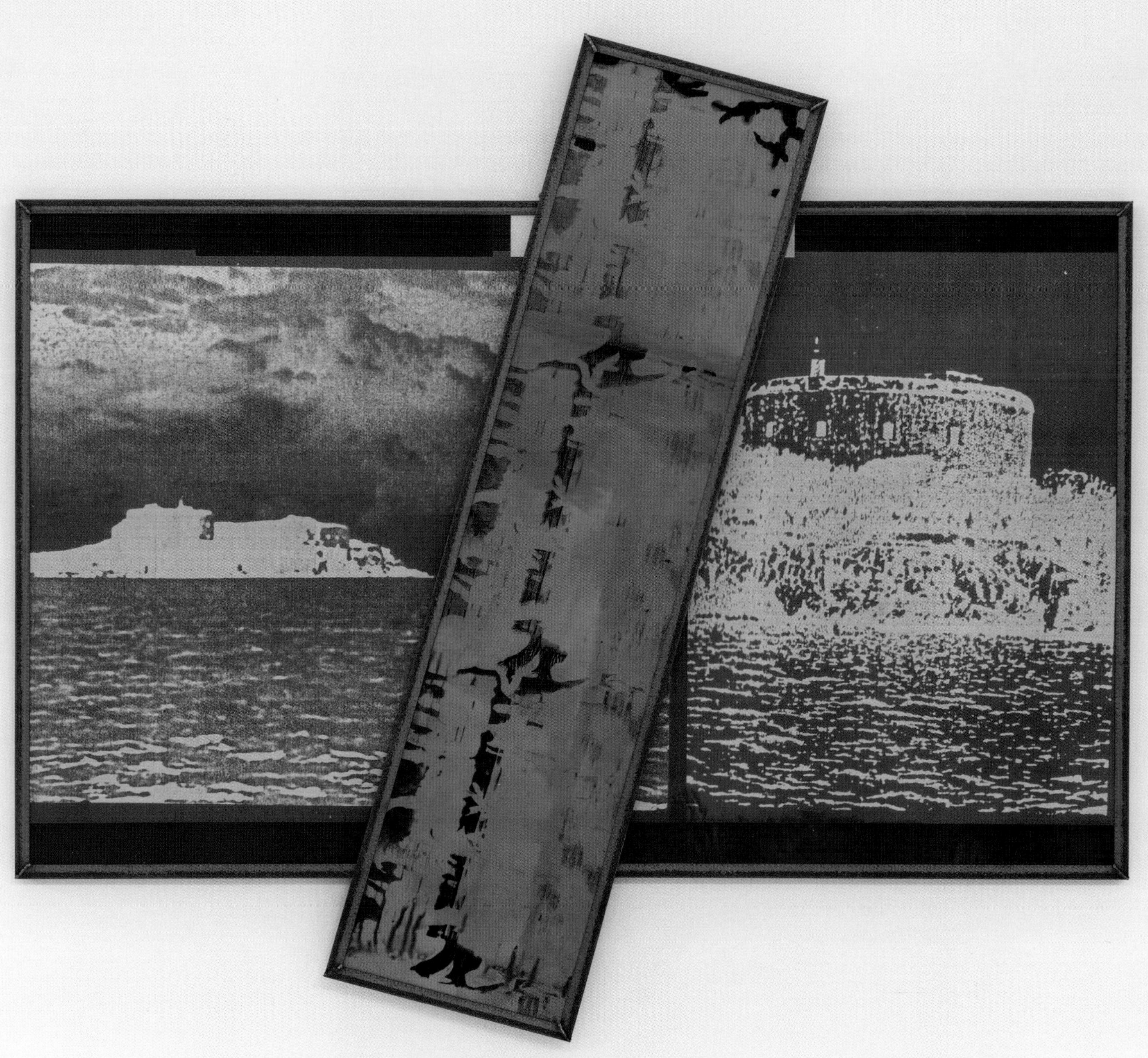

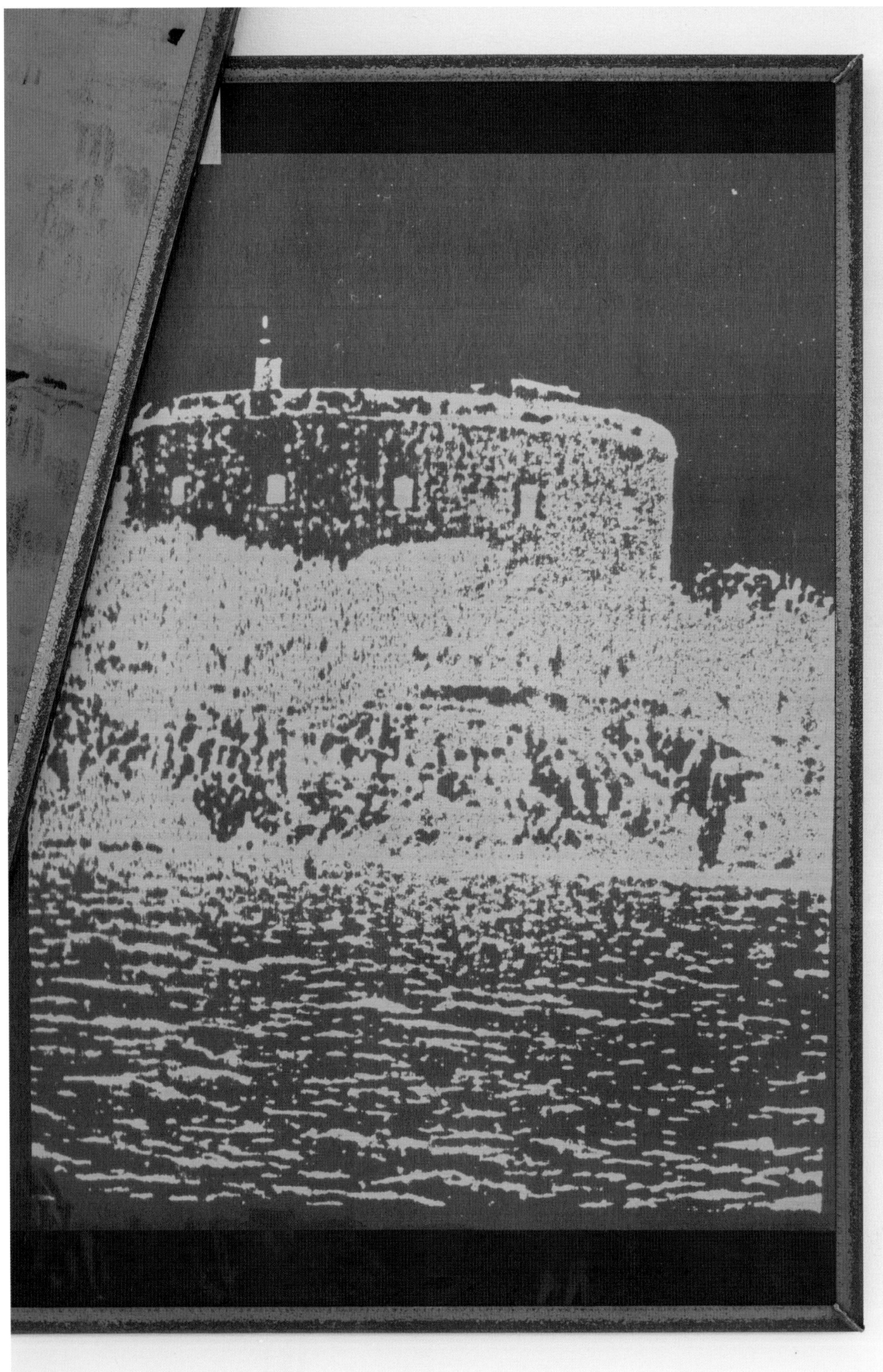

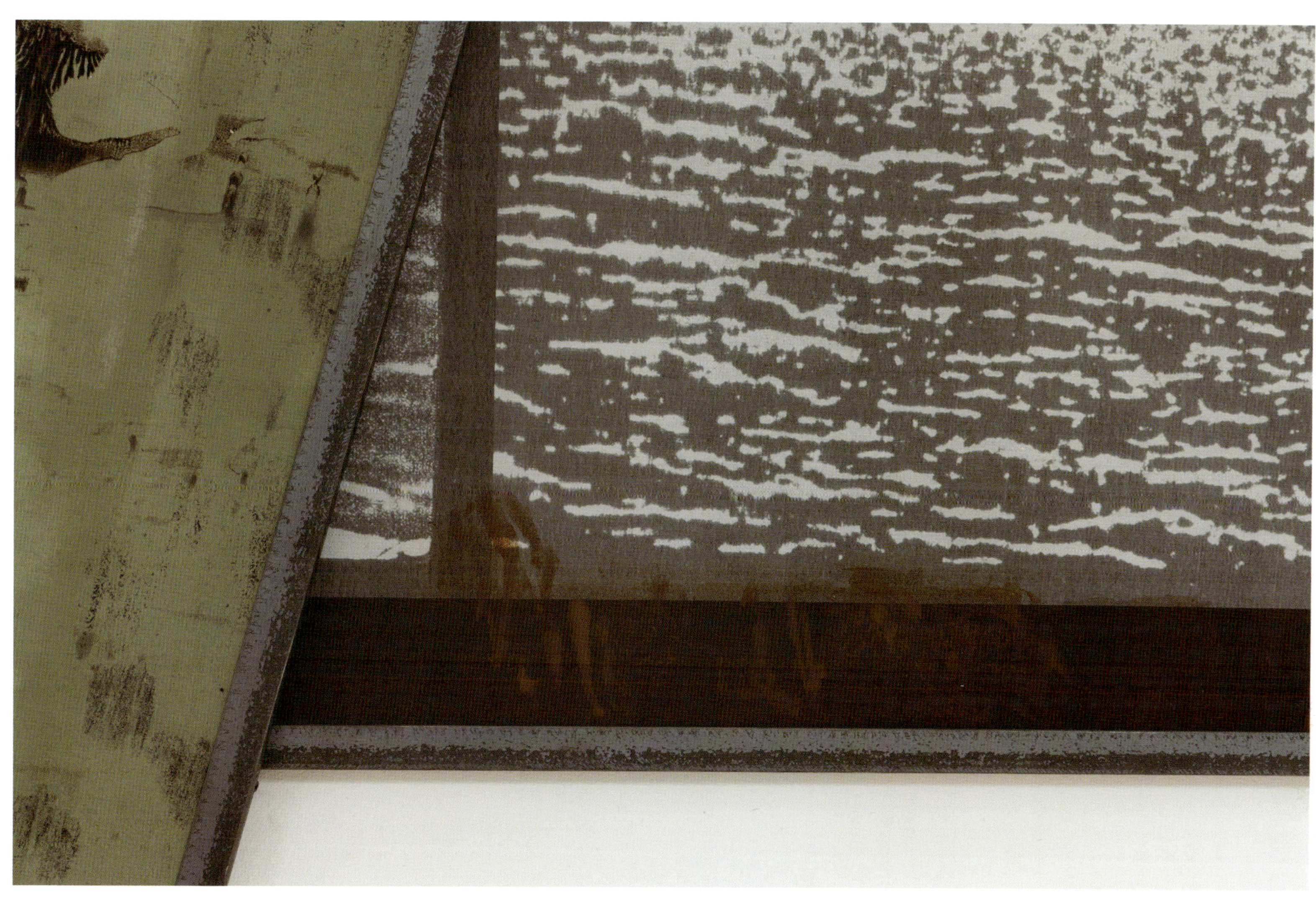

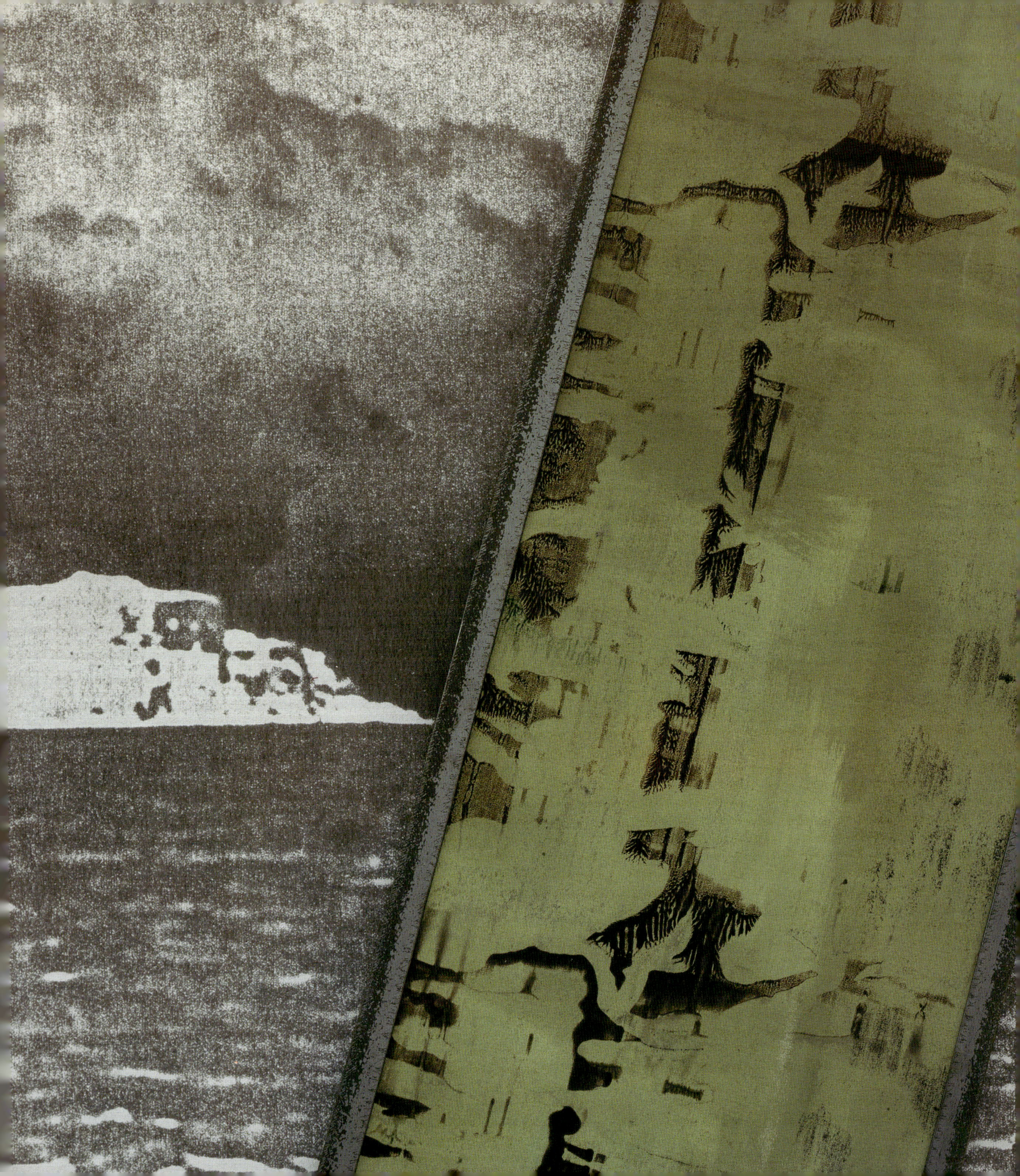

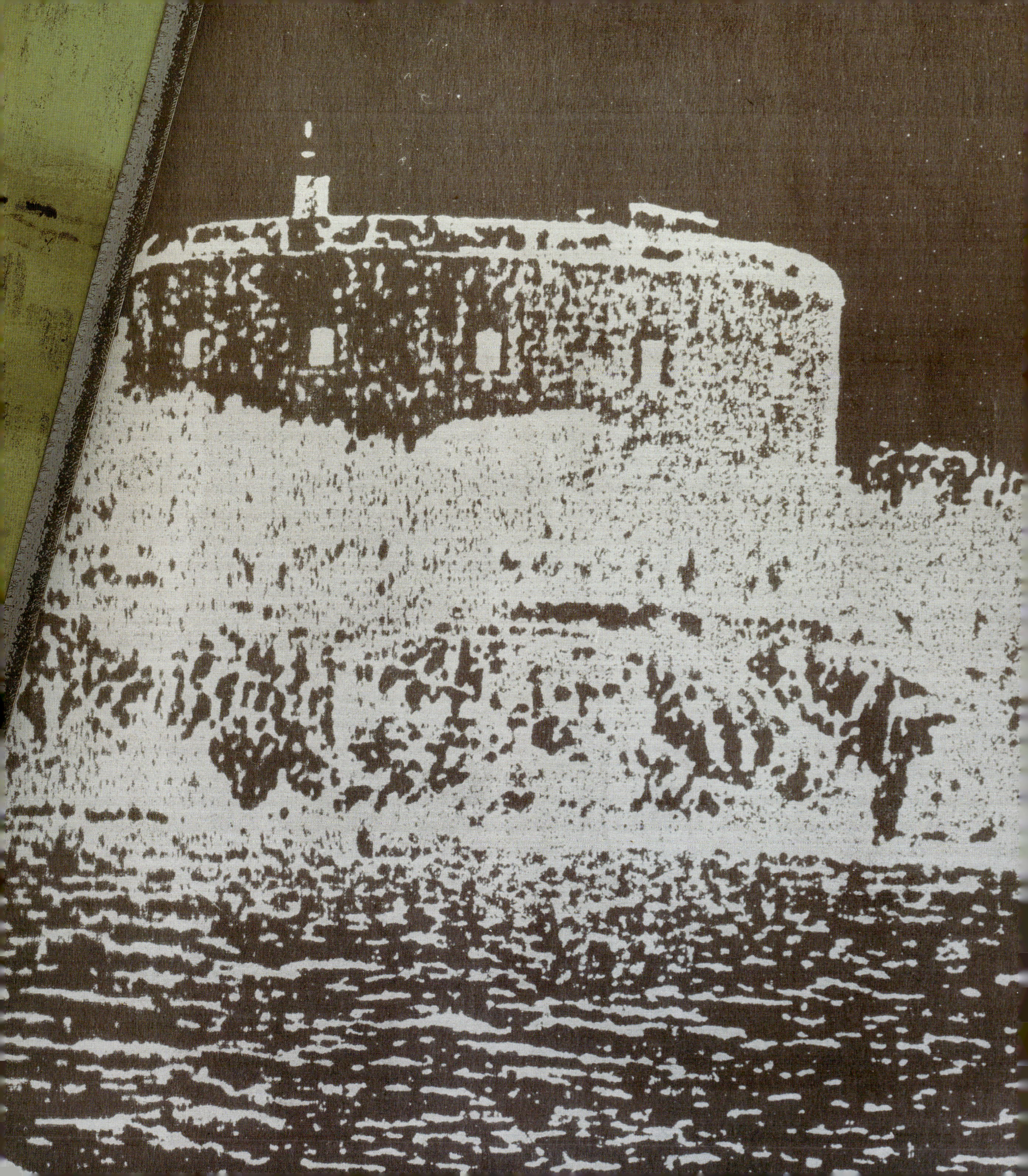

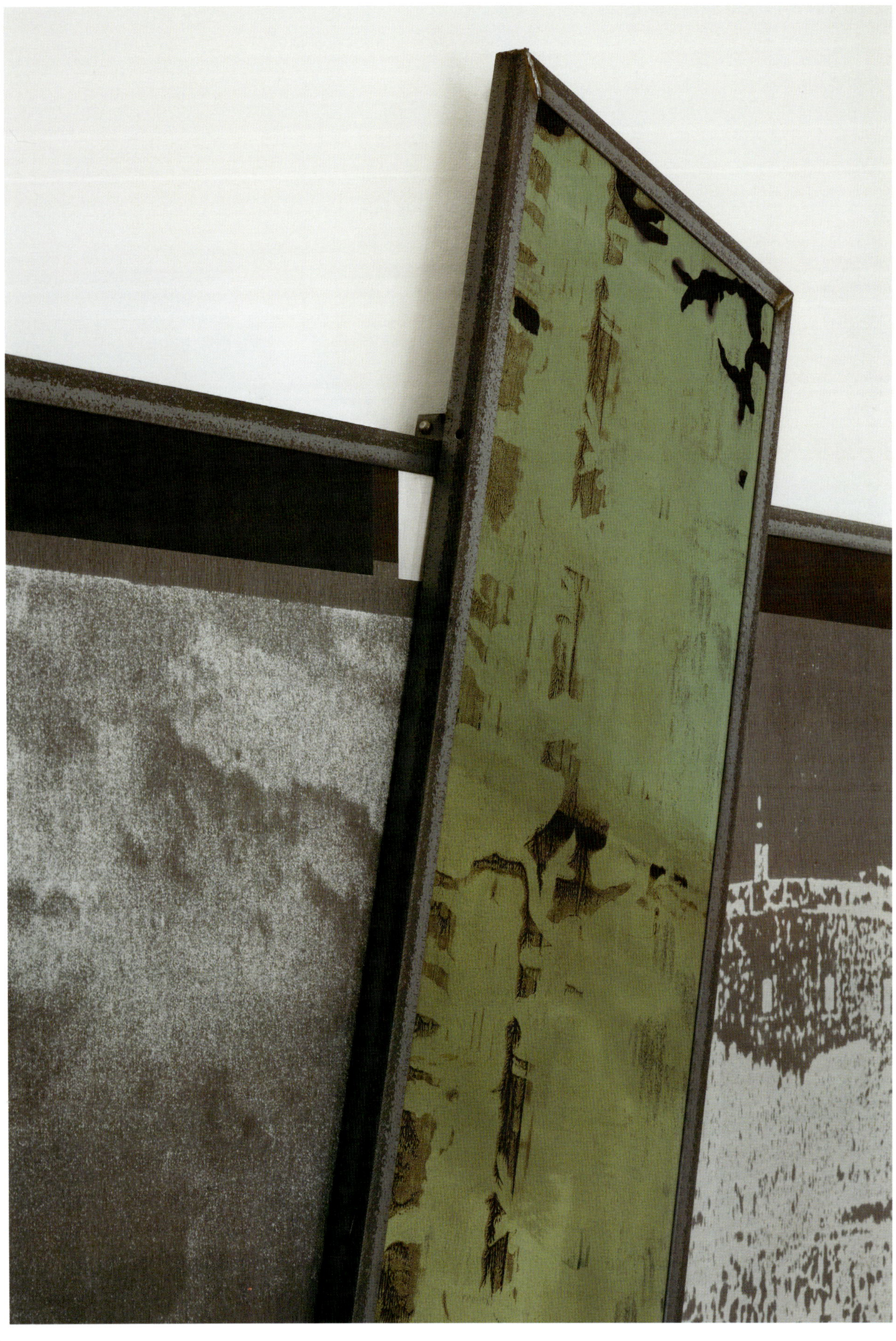

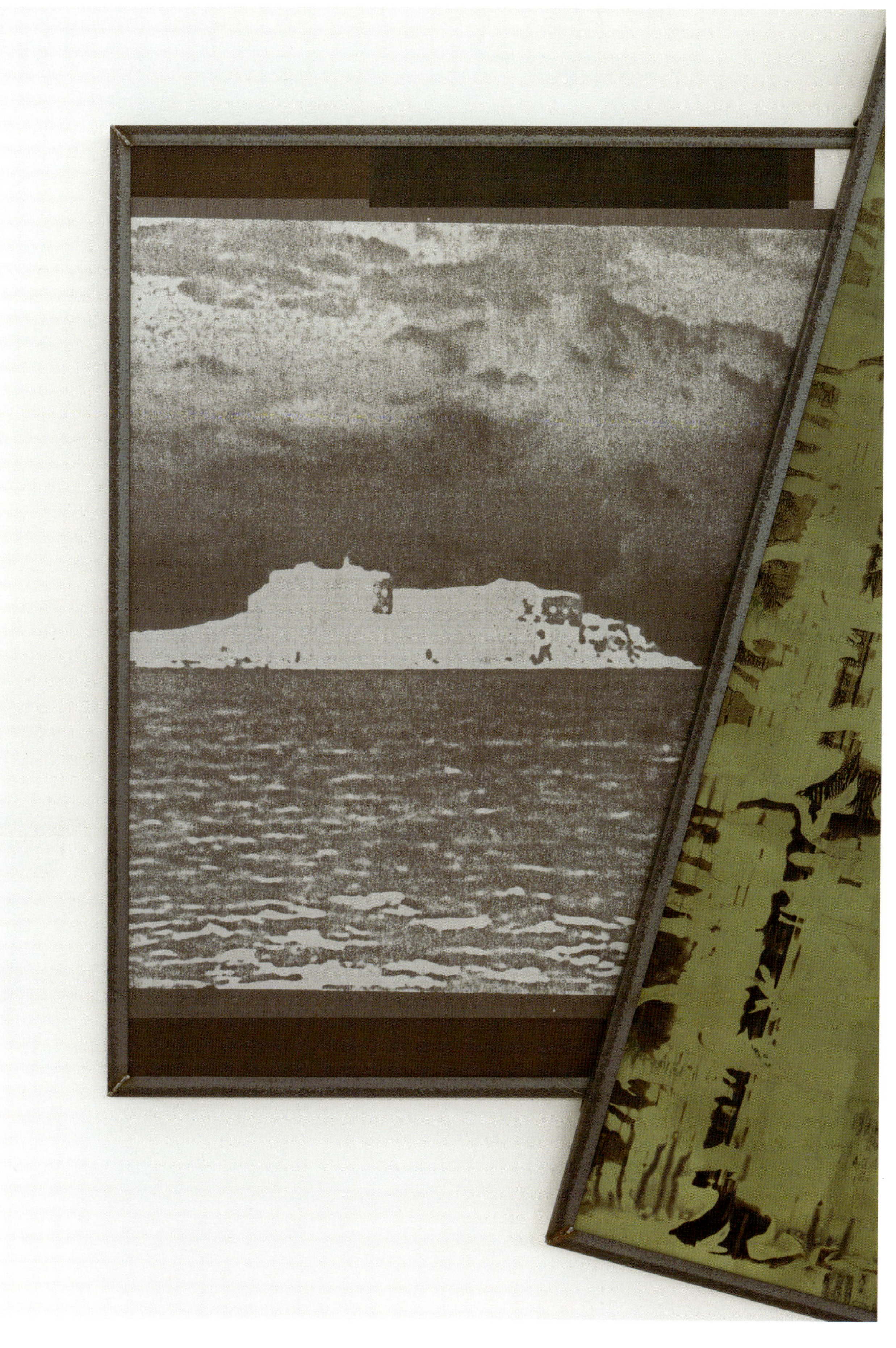

*Limb Immobilizer
(Iron Rings to Which Some
Prisoners Were Tied)*

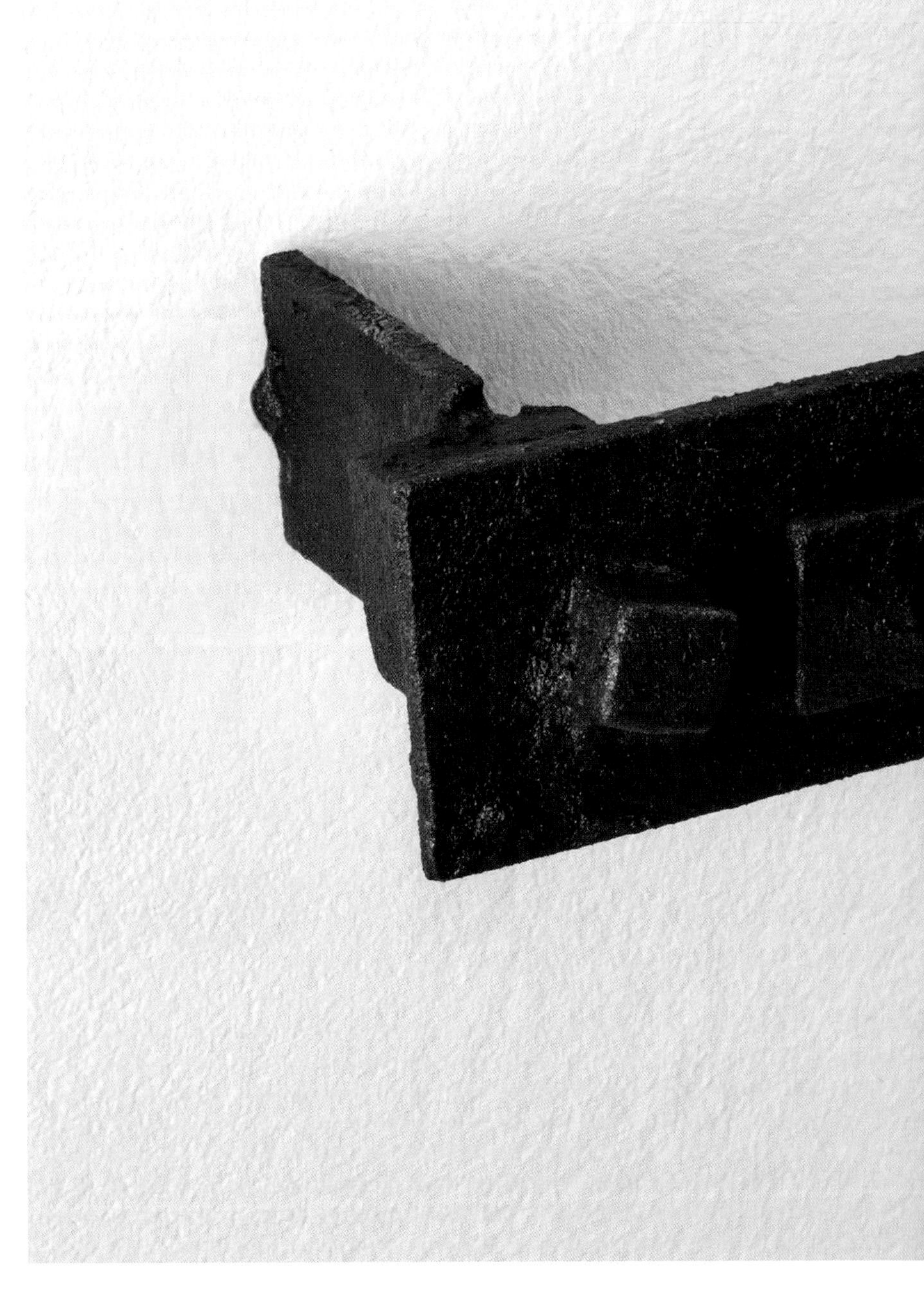

2024

Steel
Čelik

5 x 31 × 25 cm

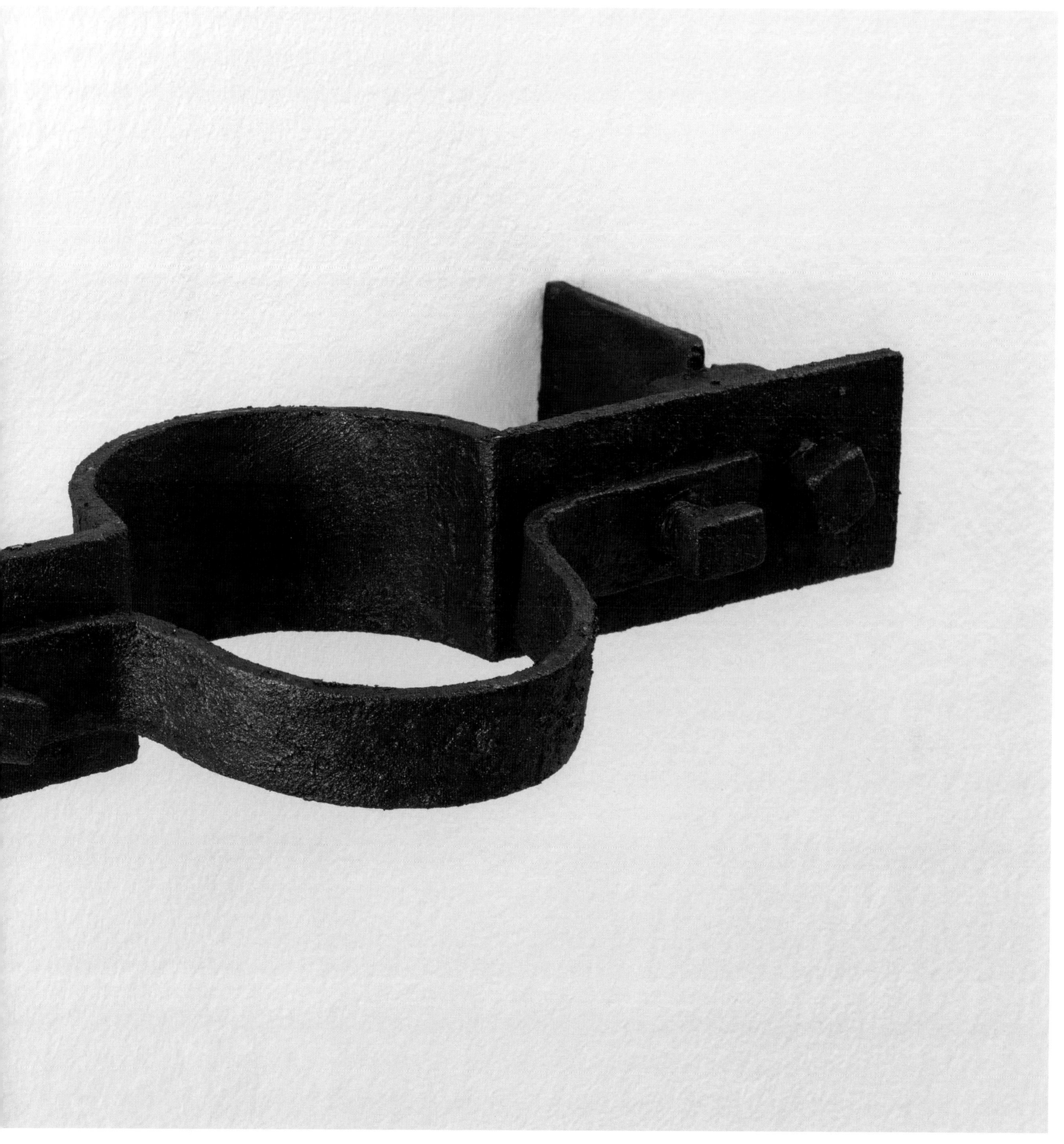

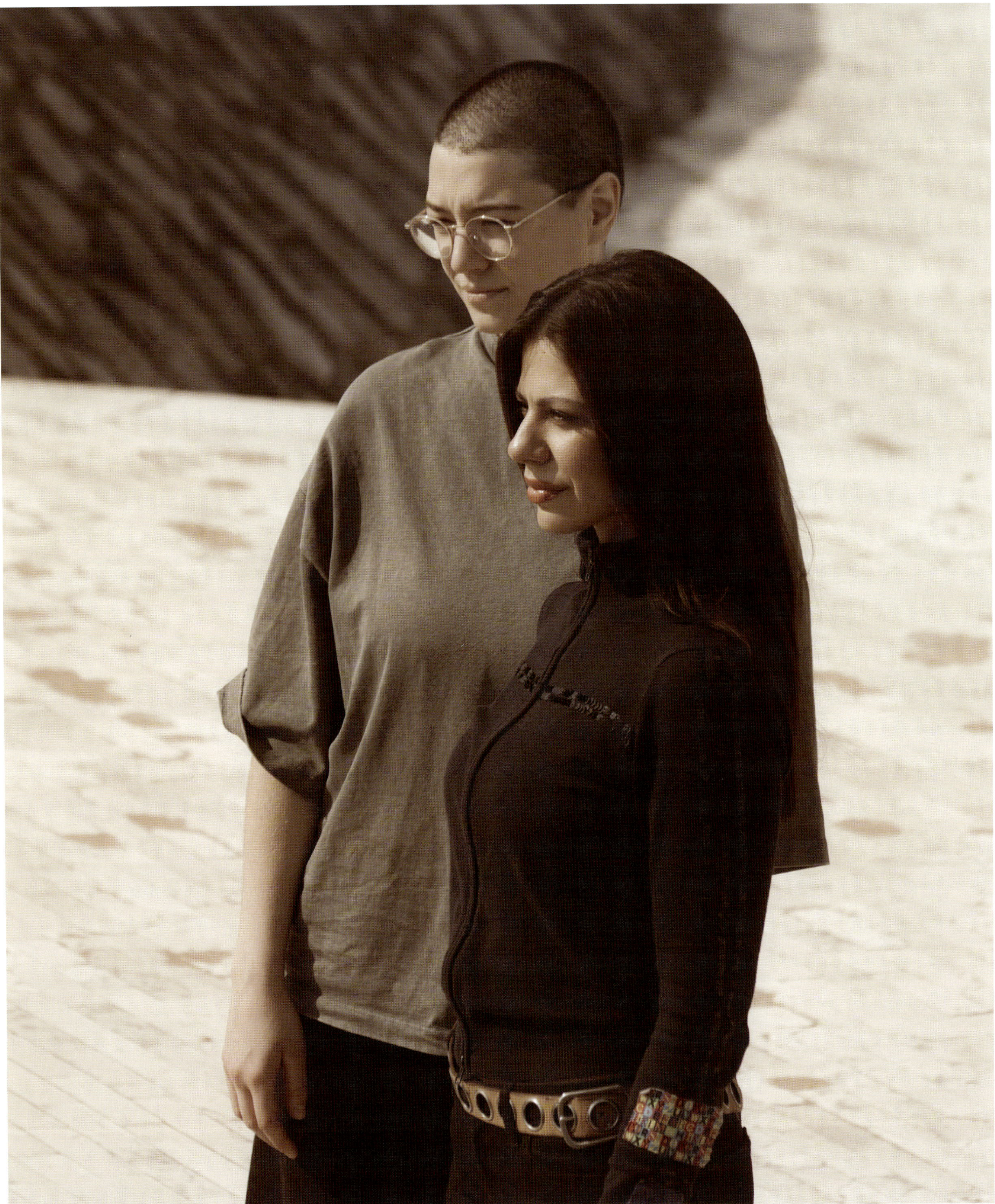

DARJA BAJAGIĆ

DARJA BAJAGIĆ

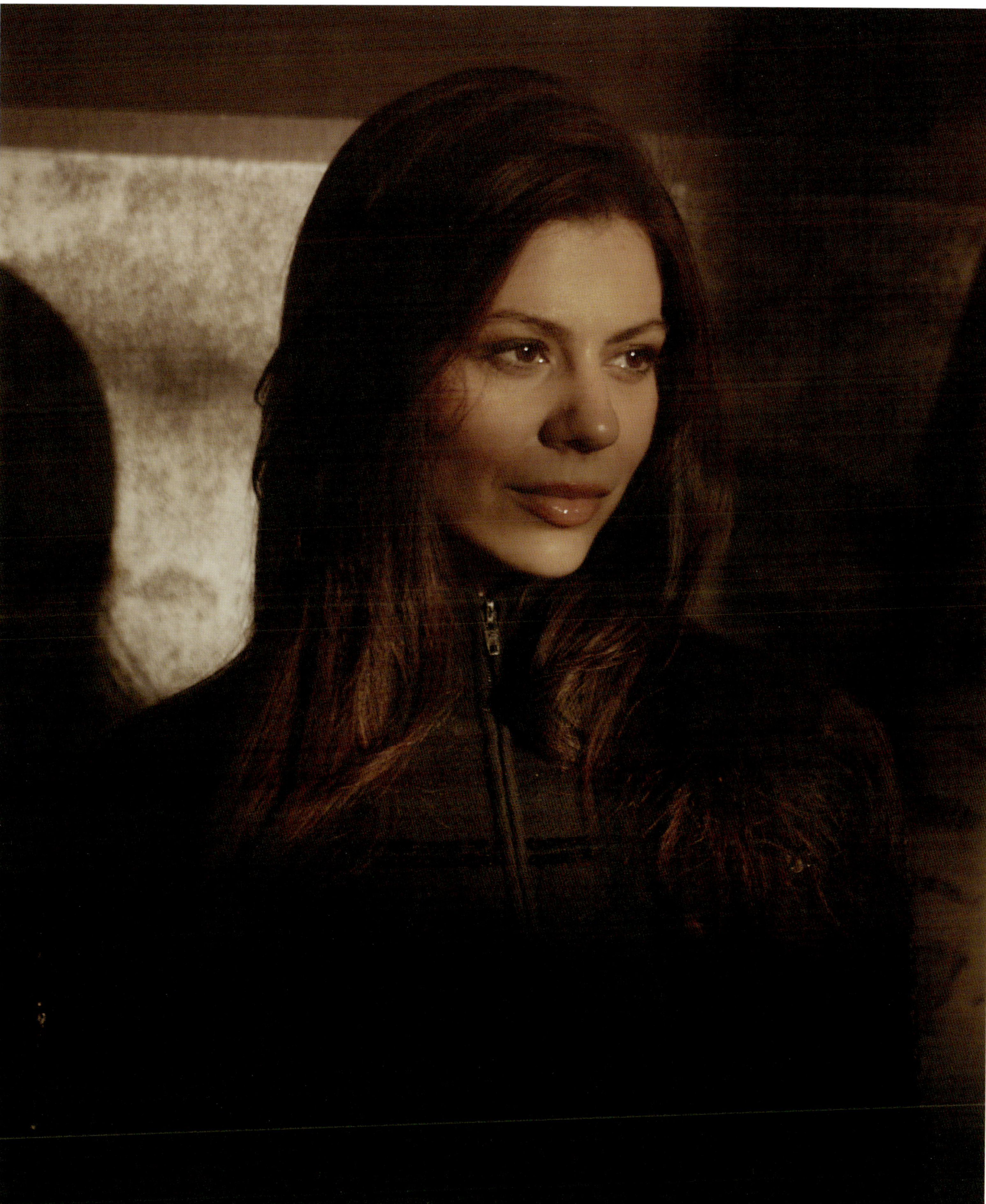

BIOGRAPHY

Darja Bajagić was born in 1990 in Podgorica, Montenegro, and raised in Egypt and the United States. She is currently based between Luštica Peninsula, Montenegro and Chicago, United States.

Bajagić received her Bachelor of Fine Arts (BFA) from the Pacific Northwest College of Art, Portland, Oregon in 2012, and her Master of Fine Arts (MFA) from the Yale University School of Art, New Haven, Connecticut in 2014, becoming the first Montenegrin national to graduate with an MFA from Yale University.

Between 2008 and 2014, during her undergraduate and graduate studies, Bajagić was a Lemelson Scholar. Lemelson Scholars are awardees of a full-tuition merit-based scholarship—granted to a single student per year who exemplifies exceptional talent and promise—funded by the Lemelson Foundation, one of Oregon's largest private foundations, with partners that include the Massachusetts Institute of Technology (MIT) and the Smithsonian Institution.

Selected institutional solo exhibitions include *Goregeous*, curated by Pierre-Alexandre Mateos and Charles Teyssou, Le Confort Moderne, Poitiers, France (2020); *Born Losers*, curated by Laura Brown, Hessel Museum of Art, Annandale-On-Hudson, New York (2018); and *Unlimited Hate*, curated by Sandro Droschl, Künstlerhaus, Halle für Kunst & Medien (KM–), Graz, Austria (2016). The catalog for *Unlimited Hate*, Bajagić's first institutional solo exhibition, was published by Sternberg Press.

Selected group exhibitions have taken place at: National Gallery Prague, Czech Republic (2021); Casino Luxembourg – Forum d'art contemporain, Luxembourg (2020); Futura Centre for Contemporary Art, Prague, Czech Republic (2019); Es Baluard Museu d'Art Contemporani de Palma, Spain (2018); Contemporary Art Centre (CAC), Vilnius, Lithuania (2018); Luma Westbau, Zürich, Switzerland (2017, 2015, 2014); Musée d'Art Moderne de Paris, France (2015); Moderna Museet, Stockholm, Sweden (2015); Museum of Modern Art in Warsaw, Poland (2014); Museo de Arte Contemporáneo de Oaxaca (MACO), Mexico (2014); Museum of Applied Arts (MAK), Vienna, Austria (2013). Most recent [group] exhibitions include *Very Friendly*, curated by Agnes Gryczkowska, at House, Berlin, Germany (2023), and *Hardcore*, curated by Sadie Coles and John O'Doherty, at Sadie Coles HQ, London, United Kingdom (2023).

Bajagić's work has been included in the 42nd Montenegrin Salon of Visual Arts, curated by Petar Ćuković, Cetinje, Montenegro (2020); the 57th October Salon, curated by Gunnar B. Kvaran and Danielle Kvaran, Belgrade, Serbia (2018); and the 13th Baltic Triennial of International Art, curated by Vincent Honoré, Vilnius, Lithuania (2018).

She has been featured in over a dozen international publications, including *Artforum International*, *Artnet*, *ARTNews*, *Autre*, *Cultured Mag*, *CURA.*, *Dazed*, *Elephant*, *Flash Art*, *Gruppe*, *i-D (Vice)*, *Interview*, *Kaleidoscope*, *L'Officiel Art*, *Les Inrockuptibles*, *Mousse*, *New American Paintings*, *The New York Times*, *Número*, *Richardson*, *Spike*, and *Vulture*.

Her work is in the public collections of EVN Sammlung, Maria Enzersdorf, Austria; Muzej savremene umjetnosti Crne Gore, Podgorica, Montenegro; KaviarFactory, Henningsvær, Norway; Museu de l'Art Prohibit, Barcelona, Spain; Es Baluard Museu d'Art Contemporani de Palma, Spain; and the Ukrainian Institute of Modern Art, Chicago, Illinois.

Bajagić is represented by Tara Downs Gallery, New York; Galleri Golsa, Oslo; and New Galerie, Paris.

CURRICULUM VITAE

BIOGRAPHY

Born 1990 in Podgorica, Montenegro
Lives and works between Luštica
    Peninsula, Montenegro and Chicago,
    United States

EDUCATION

2012–2014
Master of Fine Arts, Yale University School
    of Art, New Haven, Connecticut, United
    States

2008–2012
Bachelor of Fine Arts, Pacific Northwest
    College of Art, Portland, Oregon, United
    States

2007
Museology & Art History, The Art Institute of
    Chicago, Chicago, Illinois, United States

SELECTED SOLO EXHIBITIONS

2024
It Takes an Island to Feel This Good,
    Pavilion of Montenegro, 60th
    International Art Exhibition – La
    Biennale di Venezia, Venice, Italy

2022
Crucio, Galerija Novembar, Belgrade,
    Serbia

2020
Goregeous, Le Confort Moderne, Poitiers,
    France

2019
Transfiguration, New Galerie, Paris, France

2018
Born Losers, Hessel Museum of Art,
    Annandale-On-Hudson, New York,
    United States

2017
Damnatio Memoriae, Spazio Maiocchi,
    Milan, Italy
Darja Bajagić, presented by Carlos/
    Ishikawa, Independent New York, New
    York, New York, United States

2016
Nobody Knows I'm Funny, Carlos/Ishikawa,
    London, United Kingdom
Darja Bajagić, White Flag Library, Saint
    Louis, Missouri, United States
Unlimited Hate, Künstlerhaus, Halle für
    Kunst & Medien (KM–), Graz, Austria
Street Steve, The Window On Broad,
    Rosenwald-Wolf Gallery, The University
    of the Arts, Philadelphia, Pennsylvania,
    United States

2015
The Offal Truth, New Galerie, Paris,
    France
Diesel, Bed-Stuy Love Affair, New York,
    New York, United States

2014
C6ld c6mf6rt., Room East, New York, New
    York, United States

2013
You've Been A Naughty Boy, Appendix
    Project Space, Portland, Oregon,
    United States

SELECTED TWO-PERSON EXHIBITIONS

2022
Forest Passage with Lionel Maunz, Downs
    & Ross, New York, New York, United
    States

2020

The Banned Exhibition with Boyd Rice,
Galleri Golsa, Oslo, Norway

2019

Darja Bajagić & Andra Ursuta, presented by
Ramiken, Armory Show, New York, New
York, United States
Darja Bajagić & Sekana Radović, M.
LeBlanc, Chicago, Illinois, United States

2018

Darja Bajagić & Boyd Rice, Greenspon, New
York, New York, United States

2017

Independent Brussels, presented by
Carlos/Ishikawa, Brussels, Belgium
Darja Bajagić & Issy Wood, presented by
Carlos/Ishikawa, Independent Régence,
Brussels, Belgium

2016

Darja Bajagić & Lloyd Corporation,
presented by Carlos/Ishikawa, *Focus*
Section, Frieze London, London, United
Kingdom

2015

Softer Than Stone And Sick In Your Mind
with Aleksander Hardashnakov, Croy
Nielsen, Berlin, Germany

2014

Now Feel Bad with Jared Madere, Interstate
Projects, New York, New York, United
States

SELECTED GROUP EXHIBITIONS

2023

Very Friendly, House, Berlin, Germany
Hardcore, Sadie Coles HQ, London, United
Kingdom
Independent New York, presented by Tara
Downs, New York, New York, United
States

2022

NADA Miami, presented by Downs & Ross,
Miami, Florida, United States
Highlights, Galerija Novembar, Belgrade,
Serbia
Westbam Earthdixie, juneart.io, on-line
The American Friend, Downs & Ross, New
York, New York, United States

Body Blackout, Hamlet, Zürich, Switzerland
The Ulterior Narrative, Tick Tack, Antwerp,
Belgium
Legally Blonde, Downs & Ross, New York,
New York, United States

2021

Post-Digital Intimacy, National Gallery
Prague, Prague, Czech Republic

2020

*Noć u Crnoj Gori i druge priče, 13.
novembar*, 42. Crnogorski likovni salon
(42nd Montenegrin Salon of Visual
Arts), Miodrag Dado Đurić, Cetinje,
Montenegro
L'homme gris, Casino Luxembourg,
Luxembourg, Luxembourg
RosTA, New Galerie, Paris, France

2019

*When the time swirls, when it turns
into a black hole*, Futura Centre for
Contemporary Art, Prague, Czech
Republic
Paint, also known as Blood, Museum of
Modern Art in Warsaw, Warsaw, Poland
Orient V, Colloredo-Mansfeld Palace,
Prague, Czech Republic
Paradise, Queer Thoughts, New York, New
York, United States

2018

Hardcore Erotic Art, Ramiken, New York,
New York, United States
*False Flag: The Space Between Paranoia
and Reason*, Franklin Street Works,
Stamford, Connecticut, United States
Orient, Bunkier Sztuki, Galeria Sztuki
Współczesnej, Kraków, Poland
*The 57th October Salon, The Marvelous
Cacophony*, Belgrade City Museum,
Belgrade, Serbia
Annunciations, M. LeBlanc, Chicago,
Illinois, United States
Permanent Collection, Es Baluard Museu
d'Art Modern i Contemporani de Palma,
Palma, Spain
Putting Out, Gavin Brown's enterprise, New
York, New York, United States
Orient, BOZAR Centre for Fine Arts,
Brussels, Belgium
Orient, Kim? Contemporary Art Centre,
Rīga, Latvia
*The 13th Baltic Triennial of International Art,
Give Up The Ghost*, Contemporary Art
Centre (CAC), Vilnius, Lithuania

2017

What's Up Doc?, New Galerie, Paris, France
Transitions: Transatlantic Treatments,
Galleri Golsa, Oslo, Norway
*FADE IN 2: EXT. MODERNIST HOME –
NIGHT*, Museum of Contemporary Art,
Belgrade, Serbia, and Gallery-Legacy
of Milica Zorić & Rodoljub Čolaković,
Belgrade, Serbia
Condo New York, Bureau, New York, New
York, United States
89plus: Americans 2017, Luma Westbau,
Zürich, Switzerland
Steps to Aeration, Tanya Leighton,
Berlin, Germany
EWIG WEIBLICHE, Koppe Astner, Glasgow,
Scotland
Black Feast, Simon Lee Gallery, New York,
New York, United States

2016

Condo: Artists' Clothes, Carlos/Ishikawa,
London, United Kingdom

2015

Water from the Nile, Lodos Gallery, Mexico
City, Mexico
When Blood Runs Dark as part of *Co-
Workers*, Musée d'Art Moderne de Paris,
France
The Humane Society, The Loon, Toronto,
Canada
89plus: Filter Bubble, Luma Westbau,
Zürich, Switzerland
New Wave, Goss-Michael Foundation,
Dallas, Texas
The End of Violent Crime, Queer Thoughts,
New York, New York
True Players, W139, Amsterdam,
Netherlands
89plus: Poetry Will Be Made By All!,
Moderna Museet, Stockholm, Sweden
Where The Awning Flaps, Galerie Éric
Hussenot, Paris, France
The Subjects of the Artist, Michael
Thibault, Los Angeles, California, United
States
miart, presented by Room East, Milan, Italy
Debris, James Fuentes, New York, New
York, United States

2014

NADA Miami, presented by Room East,
Miami, Florida, United States
Seau Banco Carbon, Tomorrow Gallery, New
York, New York, United States

Spain & 42 St., Foxy Production, New York,
New York, United States
Time Remembered, William Arnold, New
York, New York, United States
Episode 14, Middlemarch, Brussels,
Belgium
New Systems, New Structures 001, William
Arnold, New York, New York, United
States
Private Settings: Art After the Internet,
Museum of Modern Art in Warsaw,
Warsaw, Poland
*Is it much too much to ask, not to hide
behind the mask?*, Old Room, New York,
New York, United States
ABNORMCORE, Room East, New York, New
York, United States
Infinitude, Roberts & Tilton, Culver City,
California, United States
Executive Producer, Museum of
Contemporary Art of Oaxaca (MACO),
Oaxaca, Mexico
USBs, Lodos Gallery, Mexico City, Mexico
89plus: Poetry will be made by all!, Luma
Westbau, Zürich, Switzerland
Partners, Lima Zulu, London, United
Kingdom
Milk of Human Kindness, Queer Thoughts,
Chicago, Illinois, United States
Alongside::D,A,K,A, Lodos Gallery, Mexico
City, Mexico

2013
Vision Quest 2013, Mana Contemporary
Chicago, Chicago, Illinois, United States
Post Internet as part of the *13festival for
fashion & photography*, Museum of
Applied Arts (MAK), Vienna, Austria
Contemporary Drawing, Forth Worth
Drawing Center, Fort Worth, Texas,
United States

2012
*I'M TOO HIGH TO DEAL WITH THIS SHIT
RIGHT NOW*, '72Truck, Madrid, Spain
SNAFU, Oliver Francis Gallery, Dallas,
Texas, United States
Sculpture Garden as part of *The Great
Poor Farm Experiment IV*, Poor Farm,
Little Wolf, Wisconsin, United States
Socks, MermHaus, Portland, Oregon,
United States

2011
Art & Leisure, Colonel Summers Park,
Portland, Oregon, United States

Aspecific Sculpture, Meat Market, Portland,
Oregon, United States

2009
Mixed: The Politics of Hybrid Identities
as part of the *6th Annual Ray Warren
Multicultural Symposium*, Lewis & Clark
College, Portland, Oregon, United
States

CONFERENCES

2013
89plus Colony Conference, moderated by
Simon Castets and Hans Ulrich Obrist,
MoMA PS1, New York, New York, United
States
Amateuring Photography [part of the
Critical Practice: Art in Conversation
conference], Yale University Art Gallery
Auditorium, New Haven, Connecticut,
United States

SELECTED CATALOGS

Crucio. Text by Ana Simona Zelenović.
Published by Galerija Novembar. 2022.

Goregeous. Texts by Pierre-Alexandre
Mateos and Charles Teyssou. Published
by Le Confort Moderne, Poitiers,
France. 2020.

Sketchbooks. Published by Kaleidoscope,
Milan, Italy. 2017.

Nobody Knows I'm Funny. Published
by Carlos/Ishikawa, London, United
Kingdom. 2017.

Unlimited Hate. Texts by Alissa Bennett,
Franklin Melendez, and Natalia
Sielewicz. Published by Sternberg
Press, London, United Kingdom. 2016.

AWARDS

2008–2014
The Lemelson Scholar Award, awarded by
the Lemelson Foundation, Portland,
Oregon, United States

PUBLIC COLLECTIONS

Austria
EVN Sammlung, Maria Enzersdorf

Montenegro
Muzej savremene umjetnosti Crne Gore,
Podgorica

Norway
KaviarFactory, Henningsvær

Spain
Museu de l'Art Prohibit, Barcelona
Es Baluard Museu d'Art Contemporani de
Palma

United States
Ukrainian Institute of Modern Art, Chicago,
Illinois

BIOGRAFIJA

Darja Bajagić je rođena 1990. godine u Podgorici, Crna Gora, a odrasla u Egiptu i Sjedinjenim Američkim Državama. Trenutno živi i radi na relaciji poluostrvo Luštica, Crna Gora i Čikago, Sjedinjene Američke Države.

Bajagić je diplomirala na akademiji likovnih umjetnosti na Pacific Northwest College of Art, Portland, Oregon 2012. godine, a magistrirala na Yale University School of Art, Nju Hejven, Konektikat 2014. godine, postavši prva državljanka Crne Gore koja je diplomirala na postdiplomskim studijama na Yale University School of Art.

U periodu od 2008. do 2014. godine, tokom osnovnih i postdiplomskih studija, Bajagić je bila Lemelson Scholar. Lemelson Scholars su dobitnici pune stipendije zasnovane na zaslugama i izuzetnom talentu i dodeljuju se jednom studentu godišnje, a finansirani su od Lemelson Foundation, koja je jedna od najvećih privatnih fondacija u Oregonu, sa partnerima koji uključuju Massachusetts Institute of Technology (MIT) i Smithsonian Institution.

Odabrane institucionalne samostalne izložbe su: *Goregeous*, kustosi Pierre-Alexandre Mateos i Charles Teyssou, Le Confort Moderne, Poatje, Francuska (2020); *Born Losers*, kustoskinja Laura Brown, Hessel Museum of Art, Annandale-On-Hudson, Nju Jork (2018); *Unlimited Hate*, kustos Sandro Droschl, Künstlerhaus, Halle für Kunst & Medien, Grac, Austrija (2016). Katalog rađen za *Unlimited Hate*, prvu Bajagićevu institucionalnu samostalnu izložbu, objavio je Sternberg Press.

Odabrane grupne izložbe održane su u: National Gallery Prague, Češka (2021); Casino Luxembourg – Forum d'art contemporain, Luksemburg (2020); Futura Centre for Contemporary Art, Prag, Češka (2019); Es Baluard Museu d'Art Contemporani de Palma, Španija (2018); Contemporary Art Centre (CAC), Vilnius, Litvanija (2018); Luma Westbau, Cirih, Švajcarska (2017, 2015, 2014); Musée d'Art Moderne de Paris, Francuska (2015); Moderna Museet, Stockholm, Švedska (2015); Museum of Modern Art in Warsaw, Poljska (2014); Museo de Arte Contemporáneo de Oaxaca (MACO), Meksiko (2014); Museum of Applied Arts (MAK), Beč, Austrija (2013). Najskorije grupne izložbe uključuju *Very Friendly*, kustoskinja Agnes Gryczkowska, u House, Berlin, Nemačka (2023), i *Hardcore*, kustosi Sadie Coles i John O'Doherty, u Sadie Coles HQ, London, Ujedinjeno Kraljevstvo (2023).

Njen rad je uvršten na 42. Crnogorskom likovnom salonu, 13. novembar, kustos Petar Ćuković, Cetinje, Crna Gora (2020); 57. Oktobarski salon, *Čudo kakofonije*, kustosi Gunnar B. Kvaran i Danielle Kvaran, Beograd, Srbija (2018); i 13. Baltičko trijenale međunarodne umjetnosti, kustos Vincent Honore, Vilnius, Litvanija (2018).

Predstavljena je u više od 10 međunarodnih publikacija uključujući *Artforum International, Artnet, ARTNews, Autre, Cultured Mag, CURA., Dazed, Elephant, Flash Art, Gruppe, i-D (Vice), Interview, Kaleidoscope, L'Officiel Art, Les Inrockuptibles, Mousse, New American Paintings, The New York Times, Número, Richardson, Spike* i *Vulture*.

Njen rad se nalazi u javnim kolekcijama EVN Sammlung, Maria Enzersdorf, Austrija; Muzej savremene umjetnosti Crne Gore, Podgorica; KaviarFactory, Henningsvær, Norveška; Museu de l'Art Prohibit, Barselona, Španija; Es Baluard Museu d'Art Contemporani de Palma, Španija; i Ukrainian Institute of Modern Art, Čikago, Ilinois.

Darju Bajagić reprezentiraju Tara Downs Gallery u Njujorku, Galleri Golsa u Oslu i New Galerie u Parizu.

CURRICULUM VITAE

BIOGRAFIJA

Rođena 1990. godine u Podgorici, Crna Gora
Živi i radi između poluostrva Luštica, Crne
  Gore i Čikaga, Sjedinjenih Američkih
  Država

OBRAZOVANJE

2012–2014.
Magistarske studije likovnih umjetnosti, Yale
  University School of Art, Nju Hejven,
  Konektikat, Sjedinjenih Američkih Država

2008–2012.
Osnovne studije likovnih umjetnosti, Pacific
  Northwest College of Art, Portland,
  Oregon, Sjedinjenih Američkih Država

2007.
Muzeologija i istorija umjetnosti, The Art
  Institute of Chicago, Čikago, Ilinoj,
  Sjedinjenih Američkih Država

ODABRANE SAMOSTALNE IZLOŽBE

2024.
It Takes an Island to Feel This Good,
  Crnogorski paviljon na 60.
  Međunarodnoj izložbi umjetnosti – La
  Biennale di Venezia, Venecija, Italija

2022.
Crucio, Galerija Novembar, Beograd, Srbija

2020.
Goregeous, Le Confort Moderne, Poatje,
  Francuska

2019.
Transfiguration, New Galerie, Pariz,
  Francuska

2018.
Born Losers, Hessel Museum of Art, Anandejl
  na Hadsonu, Njujork, Sjedinjenih
  Američkih Država

2017.
Damnatio Memoriae, Spazio Maiocchi,
  Milano, Italija
Darja Bajagić, predstavljena od Carlos/
  Ishikawa, Independent New York,
  Njujork, Sjedinjenih Američkih Država

2016.
Nobody Knows I'm Funny, Carlos/Ishikawa,
  London, Ujedinjeno Kraljevstvo
Darja Bajagić, White Flag Library, Sent Luis,
  Mizuri, Sjedinjenih Američkih Država
Unlimited Hate, Künstlerhaus, Halle für
  Kunst & Medien (KM–), Grac, Austrija
Street Steve, The Window On Broad,
  Rosenwald-Wolf Gallery, The University
  of the Arts, Philadelphia, Pensilvanija,
  Sjedinjenih Američkih Država

2015.
The Offal Truth, New Galerie, Pariz,
  Francuska
Diesel, Bed-Stuy Love Affair, Njujork,
  Njujork, Sjedinjenih Američkih Država

2014.
C6ld c6mf6rt., Room East, Njujork, Njujork,
  Sjedinjenih Američkih Država

2013.
You've Been A Naughty Boy, Appendix
  Project Space, Portland, Oregon, Njujork,
  Njujork, Sjedinjenih Američkih Država

ODABRANE KOAUTORSKE IZLOŽBE

2022.
Forest Passage sa Lionel Maunz, Downs
  & Ross, Njujork, Njujork, Sjedinjenih
  Američkih Država

2020.
The Banned Exhibition sa Boyd Rice, Galleri
Golsa, Oslo, Norveška

2019.
Darja Bajagić & Andra Ursuta, predstavljena
od Ramiken, Armory Show, Njujork,
Njujork, Sjedinjenih Američkih Država
Darja Bajagić & Sekana Radović, M. LeBlanc,
Čikago, Ilinoj, Sjedinjenih Američkih
Država

2018.
Darja Bajagić & Boyd Rice, Greenspon,
Njujork, Njujork, Sjedinjenih Američkih
Država

2017.
Independent Brussels, predstavljena od
Carlos/Ishikawa, Brisel, Belgija
Darja Bajagić & Issy Wood, predstavljena od
Carlos/Ishikawa, Independent Régence,
Brisel, Belgija

2016.
Darja Bajagić & Lloyd Corporation,
predstavljena od Carlos/Ishikawa,
Focus Section, Frieze London, London,
Ujedinjeno Kraljevstvo

2015.
Softer Than Stone And Sick In Your Mind sa
Aleksander Hardashnakov, Croy Nielsen,
Berlin, Njemačka

2014.
Now Feel Bad with Jared Madere, Interstate
Projects, Njujork, Njujork, Sjedinjenih
Američkih Država

ODABRANE GRUPNE IZLOŽBE

2023.
Very Friendly, House, Berlin, Njemačka
Hardcore, Sadie Coles HQ, London,
Ujedinjeno Kraljevstvo
Independent New York, predstavljena
od Tara Downs, Njujork, Njujork,
Sjedinjenih Američkih Država

2022.
NADA Miami, predstavljena od Downs
& Ross, Majami, Florida, Sjedinjenih
Američkih Država
Highlights, Galerija Novembar, Beograd,
Srbija

Westbam Earthdixie, juneart.io, onlajn
The American Friend, Downs & Ross,
Njujork, Njujork, Sjedinjenih Američkih
Država
Body Blackout, Hamlet, Cirih, Švajcarska
The Ulterior Narrative, Tick Tack,
Antverpen, Belgija
Legally Blonde, Downs & Ross, Njujork,
Njujork, Sjedinjenih Američkih Država

2021.
Post-Digital Intimacy, National Gallery
Prague, Prag, Češka Republika

2020.
Noć u Crnoj Gori i druge priče, 13. novembar,
42. Crnogorski likovni salon, Miodrag
Dado Đurić, Cetinje, Crna Gora
L'homme gris, Casino Luxembourg,
Luksemburg, Luksemburg
RosTA, New Galerie, Pariz, Francuska

2019.
*When the time swirls, when it turns
into a black hole*, Futura Centre for
Contemporary Art, Prag, Češka
Republika
Paint, also known as Blood, Museum of
Modern Art in Warsaw, Varšava, Poljska
Orient V, Colloredo-Mansfeld Palace, Prag,
Češka Republika
Paradise, Queer Thoughts, Njujork, Njujork,
Sjedinjenih Američkih Država

2018.
Hardcore Erotic Art, Ramiken, Njujork,
Njujork, Sjedinjenih Američkih Država
*False Flag: The Space Between Paranoia and
Reason*, Franklin Street Works, Stamford,
Konektikat, Sjedinjenih Američkih
Država
Orient, Bunkier Sztuki, Galeria Sztuki
Współczesnej, Krakov, Poljska
57. oktobarski salon, Čudo kakofonije, Muzej
grada Beograda, Beograd, Srbija
Annunciations, M. LeBlanc, Čikago, Ilinoj,
Sjedinjenih Američkih Država
Permanent Collection, Es Baluard Museu
d'Art Modern i Contemporani de Palma,
Palma, Španija
Putting Out, Gavin Brown's enterprise,
Njujork, Njujork, Sjedinjenih Američkih
Država
Orient, BOZAR Centre for Fine Arts, Brisel,
Belgija
Orient, Kim? Contemporary Art Centre,
Riga, Letonija

*The 13th Baltic Triennial of International Art,
Give Up The Ghost*, Contemporary Art
Centre (CAC), Vilnius, Litvanija

2017.
What's Up Doc?, New Galerie, Pariz,
Francuska
Transitions: Transatlantic Treatments,
Galleri Golsa, Oslo, Norveška
*FADE IN 2: EXT. MODERNIST HOME –
NIGHT*, Muzej savremene umjetnosti,
Beograd, Srbija, i Galerija-legat Milice
Zorić i Rodoljuba Čolakovića, Beograd
Srbija
Condo New York, Bureau, Njujork, Njujork,
Sjedinjenih Američkih Država
89plus: Americans 2017, Luma Westbau,
Cirih, Švajcarska
Steps to Aeration, Tanya Leighton, Berlin,
Njemačka
EWIG WEIBLICHE, Koppe Astner, Glazgov,
Škotska
Black Feast, Simon Lee Gallery, Njujork,
Njujork, Sjedinjenih Američkih Država

2016.
Condo: Artists' Clothes, Carlos/Ishikawa,
London, Ujedinjeno Kraljevstvo

2015.
Water from the Nile, Lodos Gallery, Meksiko
Siti, Meksiko
When Blood Runs Dark as part of *Co-
Workers*, Musée d'Art Moderne de Paris,
Pariz, Francuska
The Humane Society, The Loon, Toronto,
Kanada
89plus: Filter Bubble, Luma Westbau, Cirih,
Švajcarska
New Wave, Goss-Michael Foundation, Dalas,
Teksas, Sjedinjenih Američkih Država
The End of Violent Crime, Queer Thoughts,
Njujork, Njujork, Sjedinjenih Američkih
Država
True Players, W139, Amsterdam, Holandija
89plus: Poetry Will Be Made By All!, Moderna
Museet, Stokholm, Švedska
Where The Awning Flaps, Galerie Éric
Hussenot, Pariz, Francuska
The Subjects of the Artist, Michael Thibault,
Los Anđeles, Kalifornija, Sjedinjenih
Američkih Država
miart, presented by Room East, Milano,
Italija
Debris, James Fuentes, Njujork, Njujork,
Sjedinjenih Američkih Država

2014.

NADA Miami, presented by Room East,
    Majami, Florida, Sjedinjenih Američkih
    Država
Seau Banco Carbon, Tomorrow Gallery,
    Njujork, Njujork, Sjedinjenih Američkih
    Država
Spain & 42 St., Foxy Production, Njujork,
    Njujork, Sjedinjenih Američkih Država
Time Remembered, William Arnold, Njujork,
    Njujork, Sjedinjenih Američkih Država
Episode 14, Middlemarch, Brisel, Belgija
New Systems, New Structures 001, William
    Arnold, Njujork, Njujork, Sjedinjenih
    Američkih Država
Private Settings: Art After the Internet,
    Museum of Modern Art in Warsaw,
    Varšava, Poljska
*Is it much too much to ask, not to hide behind
    the mask?*, Old Room, Njujork, Njujork,
    Sjedinjenih Američkih Država
ABNORMCORE, Room East, Njujork,
    Njujork, Sjedinjenih Američkih Država
Infinitude, Roberts & Tilton, Kalver Siti,
    Kalifornija, Sjedinjenih Američkih
    Država
Executive Producer, Museum of
    Contemporary Art of Oaxaca (MACO),
    Oahaka, Meksiko
USBs, Lodos Gallery, Meksiko Siti, Meksiko
89plus: Poetry will be made by all!, Luma
    Westbau, Cirih, Švajcarska
Partners, Lima Zulu, London, Ujedinjeno
    Kraljevstvo
Milk of Human Kindness, Queer Thoughts,
    Čikago, Ilinoj, Sjedinjenih Američkih
    Država
Alongside::D,A,K,A, Lodos Gallery, Meksiko
    Siti, Meksiko

2013.

Vision Quest 2013, Mana Contemporary
    Chicago, Čikago, Ilinoj, Sjedinjenih
    Američkih Država
Post Internet as part of the *13festival for
    fashion & photography*, Museum of
    Applied Arts (MAK), Beč, Austrija
Contemporary Drawing, Forth Worth
    Drawing Center, Fort Worth, Teksas,
    Sjedinjenih Američkih Država

2012.

*I'M TOO HIGH TO DEAL WITH THIS SHIT
    RIGHT NOW*, '72Truck, Madrid, Španija
SNAFU, Oliver Francis Gallery, Dalas,
    Teksas, Sjedinjenih Američkih Država

Sculpture Garden as part of *The Great Poor
    Farm Experiment IV*, Poor Farm, Litl
    Vulf, Viskonsin, Sjedinjenih Američkih
    Država
Socks, MermHaus, Portland, Oregon,
    Sjedinjenih Američkih Država

2011.

Art & Leisure, Colonel Summers Park,
    Portland, Oregon, Sjedinjenih Američkih
    Država
Aspecific Sculpture, Meat Market, Portland,
    Oregon, Sjedinjenih Američkih Država

2009.

Mixed: The Politics of Hybrid Identities
    as part of the *6th Annual Ray Warren
    Multicultural Symposium*, Lewis & Clark
    College, Portland, Oregon, Sjedinjenih
    Američkih Država

KONFERENCIJE

2013.

89plus Colony Conference, moderatori Simon
    Castets i Hans Ulrich Obrist, MoMA PS1,
    Njujork, Njujork, Sjedinjenih Američkih
    Država
Amateuring Photography [u okviru projekta
    Critical Practice: Art in Conversation
    conference], Yale University Art Gallery
    Auditorium, Nju Hejven, Konektikat,
    Sjedinjenih Američkih Država

ODABRANI KATALOZI

Crucio. Tekst Ana Simona Zelenović. Izdavač
    Galerija Novembar. 2022.

Goregeous. Tekstovi Pierre-Alexandre Mateos
    i Charles Teyssou. Izdavač Le Confort
    Moderne, Poatje, Francuska. 2020.

Sketchbooks. Izdavač Kaleidoscope, Milano,
    Italija. 2017.

Nobody Knows I'm Funny. Izdavač Carlos/
    Ishikawa, London, Ujedinjeno
    Kraljevstvo. 2017.

Unlimited Hate. Tekstovi Alissa Bennett,
    Franklin Melendez, i Natalia Sielewicz.
    Izdavač Sternberg Press, London,
    Ujedinjeno Kraljevstvo. 2016.

NAGRADE

2008–2014

Nagrada Lemelson Scholar Award, koju
    dodeljuje Lemelson Foundation,
    Portland, Oregon, Sjedinjenih Američkih
    Država

JAVNE KOLEKCIJE

Austrija
EVN Sammlung, Maria Enzersdorf

Crna Gora
Muzej savremene umjetnosti Crne Gore,
    Podgorica

Norveška
KaviarFactory, Henningsvær

Španija
Museu de l'Art Prohibit, Barcelona
Es Baluard Museu d'Art Contemporani de
    Palma

SAD
Ukrainian Institute of Modern Art, Čikago,
    Ilinoj

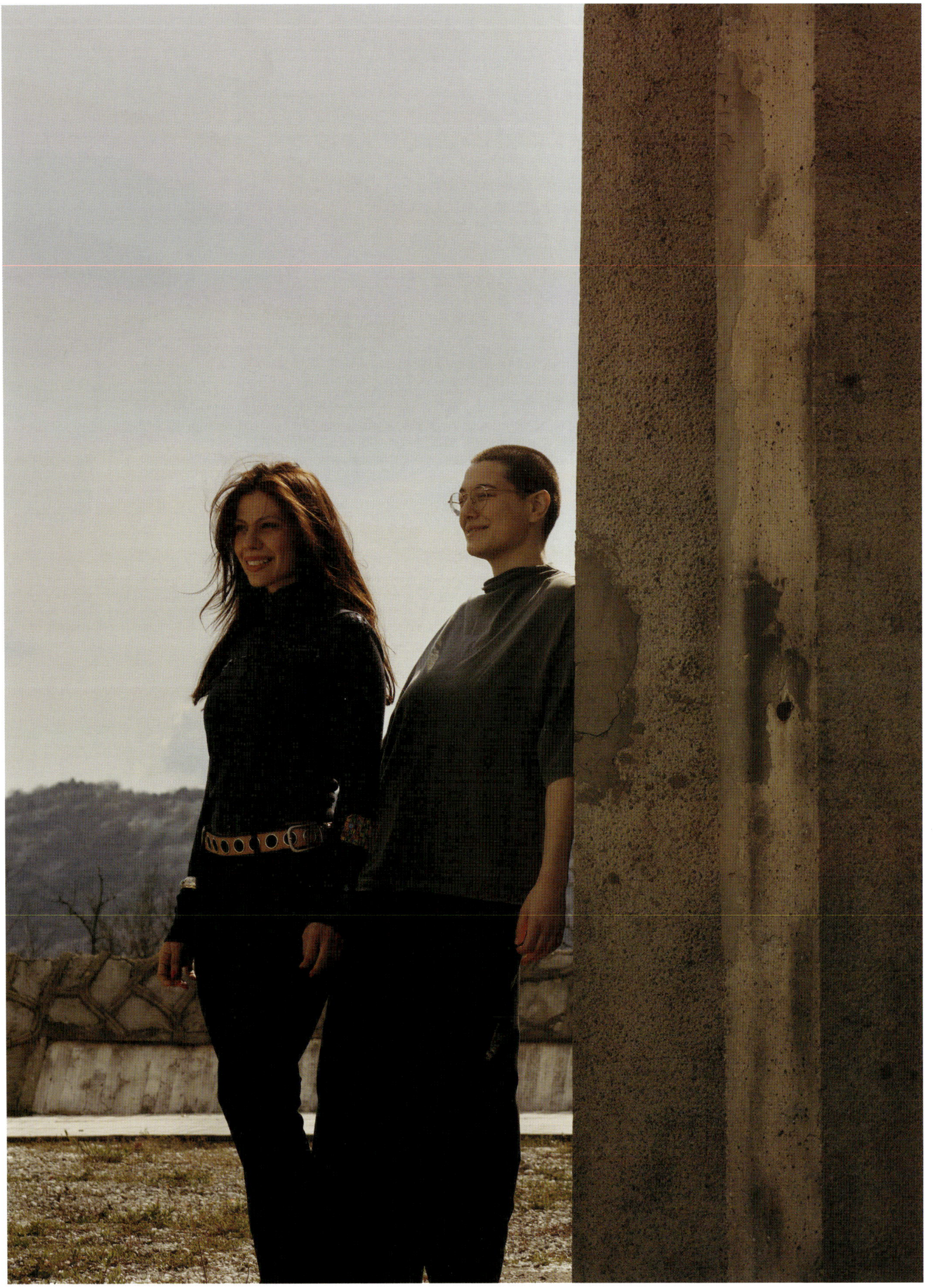

ANA SIMONA
ZELENOVIĆ

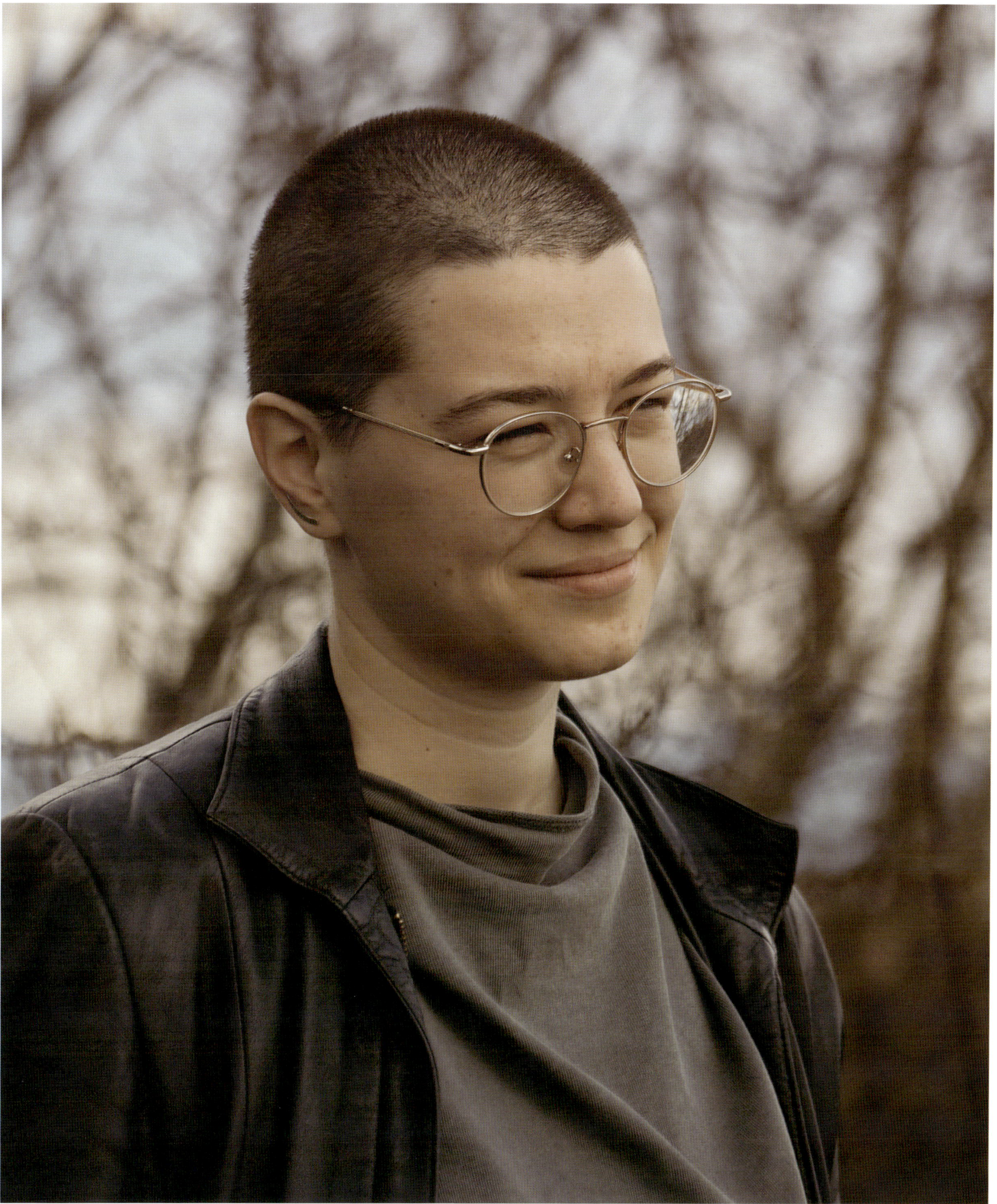

BIOGRAPHY

Ana Simona Zelenović is an art historian and curator based in Belgrade, Serbia. In 2021, she was appointed as the art director and head curator of Galerija Novembar, Belgrade, where she worked until 2024.

Zelenović holds a Bachelor of Arts (2015) and Master of Arts (2017) in art history from the University of Belgrade Faculty of Philosophy and a Master of Arts (2019) in gender studies from the University of Belgrade Faculty of Political Science. Currently, she is a doctoral candidate at the University of Belgrade Faculty of Philosophy in the Department of Art History. Her thesis investigates the history of feminist performance art in former Yugoslavia and Serbia. Supplementing her interest in and research of constructivist approaches to understanding gender identity, sexual orientation, and sexuality, she simultaneously studies constructivist psychotherapy at PLK Centar (PLK is an acronym for Psihologija Ličnih Konstrukata, or Psychology of Personal Constructs), Belgrade.

In her practice, she uses an intersectional feminist approach to investigate, analyze, and curate art, focusing on feminist and queer aesthetics and culture. In collaboration with various feminist organizations, she curates exhibitions that explore and concentrate on the position and representation of women, gender, and sexuality.

She is co-founder of *SELFI* Magazine, an annual print journal dedicated to women artists, and a contributing writer for *Numéro Berlin*.

CURRICULUM VITAE

BIOGRAPHY

Born 1993 in Kraljevo, Serbia
Lives and works in Belgrade, Serbia

EDUCATION

2020–present
Diploma in Constructivist Psychotherapy,
PLK Centar, Belgrade, Serbia

2018–present
Doctoral Candidate, Art History, University
of Belgrade Faculty of Philosophy,
Belgrade, Serbia

2017–2019
Master of Arts, Gender Studies, University
of Belgrade Faculty of Political Science,
Belgrade, Serbia

2015–2017
Master of Arts, Art History, University
of Belgrade Faculty of Philosophy,
Belgrade, Serbia

2011–2015
Bachelor of Arts, Art History, University
of Belgrade Faculty of Philosophy,
Belgrade, Serbia

SELECTED WORK EXPERIENCE

2023–2025
Council Member of the Artist Changemaker
program, Global Fund for Women, San
Francisco, California, United States

2021–present
Contributing Writer, *Numéro Berlin*, Berlin,
Germany

2021–present
Co-Founder, Co-Editor, Contributing Writer,
SELFI Magazine, Belgrade, Serbia

2021–2024
Art Director and Head Curator, Galerija
Novembar, Belgrade, Serbia

2017–present
External Associate, BeFem, Belgrade,
Serbia

2016–present
Independent Curator

2016–present
Art Critic, *MILICA Magazine*, Belgrade,
Serbia

2019–2020
Curatorial Assistant, Galerija Novembar,
Belgrade, Serbia

2019–2020
Contributing Reporter, Remarker Media,
Belgrade, Serbia

2019
Project Manager, Heartefact, Belgrade,
Serbia

SELECTED CURATORIAL PROJECTS

2024
Curator, Darja Bajagić, *It Takes an Island to
Feel This Good*, Pavilion of Montenegro,
60th International Art Exhibition – La
Biennale di Venezia

2023
Curator, *Arcadia*, Queer Museum Vienna,
Vienna, Austria

2022

Curatorial Assistant, *Feminist Avant-Garde*, Museum of Contemporary Art of Vojvodina, Novi Sad, Serbia

2022

Curator, *The Art of Anti-War*, Center for Cultural Decontamination (CZKD), Belgrade, Serbia

2021

Curator, *The Art of Anti-War*, Historical Museum of Bosnia and Herzegovina, Sarajevo, Bosnia and Herzegovina

2021

Curator, *Under Your Skin*, Femix Festival, Cultural Center of Belgrade (KCB) and Magacin Cultural Center (MKM), Belgrade, Serbia

2018

Curatorial Assistant, Oktobarski Salon, Belgrade Biennale, Belgrade, Serbia

2018

Curator, *Queer Salon*, Termokiss, Prishtina, Kosovo

2017

Curator, *Queer Salon*, European Centre for Culture and Debate (KC Grad), Belgrade, Serbia

2017

Curator, *Gender Expression*, Serbian Green Youth, Magacin Cultural Center (MKM), Belgrade, Serbia

SELECTED LECTURES, ROUNDTABLES, AND WORKSHOPS

2022

Roundtable Moderator, *Gender-based Violence*, Pride Info Center, Belgrade, Serbia

2021

Workshop Lecturer, *What is Queer Art?*, Pride Info Center, Belgrade, Serbia

2021

Roundtable Moderator, *Defenders of Women's Right in Art*, BeFem Talks, Kafe Bar 16, Belgrade, Serbia

2020

Lecturer, *Feminist & Queer Art in SFRY*, Pride Info Center, Belgrade, Serbia

2020

Roundtable Moderator, *Visual Representation and Typologization of Queer Identities*, Pride Week Community Talks, Pride Info Center, Belgrade, Serbia

2019

Roundtable Moderator, *Second Sex: First Encounters With the Book*, Institute for Philosophy and Social Theory (IFDT), University of Belgrade, Belgrade, Serbia

2017

Workshop Lecturer, *Identifying Intersections Between ROMA and LGBTQI Communities*, Tirana, Albania

2016

Roundtable Moderator, *Feminism in Pop Culture*, Serbian Green Youth, Magacin Cultural Center (MKM), Belgrade, Serbia

SELECTED PUBLICATIONS

Zelenović, Ana Simona. 2020. *Theorization of Feminist Art in Socialist Yugoslavia*. Genero no. 23. Belgrade: Faculty of Political Sciences and Center for Women's Studies.

Zelenović, Ana Simona. 2017. *Considering the Possibility of Characterizing the Illuminated*

Forms of Vojin Bakić as Minimalist Art. Kultura. no. 155. Belgrade: Institute for Cultural Development. pp. 266–277.

Zelenović, Ana Simona. 2018. *An Analysis and Interpretation of the Performance Art, Happenings, and Body Art of Katalin Ladik: A Feminist Study*. Genero no. 22. Belgrade: Faculty of Political Sciences and Center for Women's Studies. pp. 113–141.

Zelenović, Ana Simona. 2021. *Architecture in Zenit Magazine*. Literary History — Journal of Literary Studies. vol. 53. no. 175. pp. 234–253.

AWARDS AND SCHOLARSHIPS

2021

BeFem Award for Peace Building Through Art for the exhibition *The Art of Anti-War*, Historical Museum of Bosnia and Herzegovina, Sarajevo, Bosnia and Herzegovina

2017–19

Žarana Papić Scholarship for Master of Arts, Gender Studies, University of Belgrade Faculty of Political Science, Belgrade, Serbia

BIOGRAFIJA

Ana Simona Zelenović je istoričarka umjetnosti i kustoskinja koja živi i radi u Beogradu, Srbija. Godine 2021. imenovana je za umjetničku direktorku i glavnu kustoskinju Novembar galerije u Beogradu gdje je radila do 2024.

Zelenović je diplomirala (2015) i masterirala (2017) istoriju umjetnosti na Filozofskom fakultetu Univerziteta u Beogradu i masterirala studije roda (2019) na Fakultetu političkih nauka Univerziteta u Beogradu. Doktorantkinja je na istoriji umjetnosti na Filozofskom fakultetu Univerziteta u Beogradu, a u svojoj tezi se bavi feminističkim performansom u Jugoslaviji i Srbiji. Dopunjuje svoje interesovanje i istraživanje konstruktivističkih pristupa rodu i seksualnosti istovremeno pohađajući edukaciju iz konstruktivističke psihoterapije u PLK Centru (Psihologija ličnih konstrukata) u Beogradu.

U svojoj praksi koristi intersekcionalni feministički pristup istraživanju, analiziranju i kustosiranju umjetnosti.

Suosnivačica je godišnjaka *SELFI* (Beograd, Srbija), koji je posvećen ženskoj umjetničkoj produkciji i kritici i istovremeno piše za umjetnički časopis *Numéro Berlin*, (Berlin, Nemačka).

CURRICULUM VITAE

BIOGRAFIJA

Rođena 1993 u Kraljevu, Srbija
Živi i radi u Beogradu, Srbija

OBRAZOVANJE

2020–sad
Konstruktivistička psihoterapija, PLK
Centar, Beograd, Srbija

2018–sad
Doktorantkinja, Istorija umjetnosti,
Univerzitet u Beogradu Filozofski
fakultet, Beograd, Srbija

2017–2019
Master politikološkinja, Rodne studije,
Fakultet političkih nauka, Univerzitet u
Beogradu, Srbija

2015–2017
Master istoričarka umjetnosti, Filozofski
fakultet, Univerzitet u Beogradu, Srbija

2011–2015
Osnovne studije, Istorija umjetnosti,
Filozofski fakultet, Univerzitet u
Beogradu, Srbija

ODABRANO RADNO ISKUSTVO

2023–2025
Članica Savjeta za Artist Changemaker
program, Global Fund for Women, San
Francisko, Kalifornia, SAD

2021–sad
Dopisnica, *Numéro Berlin*, Berlin, Nemačka

2021–sad
Suosnivačica, autorka i urednica, *SELFI*
Magazin, Beograd, Srbija

2021–2024
Umjetnička direktorka i kustoskinja, Galerija
Novembar, Beograd, Srbija

2017–sad
Spoljna saradnica, BeFem, Beograd, Srbija

2016–sad
Nezavisna kustoskinja

2019–2020
Likovna kritičarka, *MILICA Magazin*,
Beograd, Srbija

2019–2020
Asistentkinja kustosa, Galerija Novembar,
Beograd, Srbija

2019–2020
Dopisnica, Remarker Media, Beograd, Srbija

2019
Projektna menadžerka, Heartefact, Beograd,
Srbija

ODABRANI KUSTOSKI PROJEKTI

2024
Kustoskinja, Darja Bajagić, *It Takes an Island
to Feel This Good*, Crnogorski paviljon na
60. Međunarodnoj izložbi umjetnosti –
La Biennale di Venezia, Venecija, Italija

2023
Kustoskinja, *Arcadia*, Queer Museum
Vienna, Beč, Austrija

2022
Saradnica, *Feminist Avant-Garde*, Muzej
savremene umetnosti Vojvodine (MSUV),
Novi Sad, Srbija

2022
Kustoskinja, *Umetnost Antirata*, Centar
za kulturnu dekontaminaciju (CZKD),
Beograd, Srbija

2021
Kustoskinja, *Umetnost Antirata*, Historijski
muzej Bosne i Hercegovine, Sarajevo,
Bosna i Hercegovina

2021
Kustoskinja, *Under Your Skin*, Femix
Festival, Kulturni Centar Beograda (KCB)
i Magacin (MKM), Beograd, Srbija

2018
Saradnica, Oktobarski Salon, Belgrade
Biennale, Beograd, Srbija

2018
Kustoskinja, *Queer Salon*, Termokiss,
Priština, Kosovo

2017
Kustoskinja, *Queer Salon*, KC Grad, Beograd,
Srbija

2017
Kustoskinja, *Gender Expression*, Zelena
Omladina Srbije, Magacin (MKM),
Belograd, Srbija

**ODABRANA PREDAVANJA, OKRUGLI
STOLOVI I RADIONICE**

2022
Moderatorka razgovora, *Nasilje u istopolnim
zajednicama*, Pride Info Center, Beograd,
Srbija

2021
Radionica i predavanje, *What is Queer Art?*,
Pride Info Center, Beograd, Srbija

2021

Moderatorka razgovora, *Ljudska prava u umetnosti*, BeFem Talks, Kafe Bar 16, Belgrade, Srbija

2020

Predavanje, *Feministička & Kvir umetnost* u SFRJ, Pride Info Center, Beograd, Srbija

2020

Predavanje, *Vizuelna reprezentacija kvir identiteta*, Pride Week Community Talks, Pride Info Center, Beograd, Srbija

2019

Učesnica panela, *Drugi pol: Prvi susret sa knjigom*, Institut za filozofiju i društvenu teoriju (IFDT), Univerzitet u Beogradu, Srbija

2017

Predavanje na panelu, *Intersekcija između romskih i LGBTQI zajednica*, Tirana, Albanija

2016

Moderatorka, *Feminizam u pop kulturi*, Zelena Omladina Srbije, Magacin (MKM), Beograd, Srbija

ODABRANE PUBLIKACIJE

Zelenović, Ana Simona. 2020. *Teoretizacija feminističke umetnosti u socijalističkoj Jugoslaviji*. Genero no. 23. Beograd: Fakultet političkih nauka i Centar za ženske studije. str. 71–111

Zelenović, Ana Simona. 2017. *Mogućnosti razmatranja karakterizacije Svetlosnih formi Vojina Bakića kao Milimal Art-a*. Kultura. no. 155. Beograd: Institut za kulturni razvoj. str. 266–277.

Zelenović, Ana Simona. 2018. *Analiza i interpretacija performansa, hepeninga i body art-a Katalin Ladik: Feministička studija. Genero no. 22. Beograd: Fakultet političkih nauka i Centar za ženske studije.* str. 113–141.

Zelenović, Ana Simona. 2021. *Arhitektura u časopisu Zenit*. Književna istorija - Časopis za nauku o književnosti. vol. 53. no. 175. str. 234–253.

NAGRADE I STIPENDIJE

2021

BeFem Nagrada za izgradnju mira kroz umjetnost za izložbu *Umetnost Antirata*, Historijski Muzej Bosne i Hercegovine, Sarajevo, BiH

2017–2019

Žarana Papić Stipendija za Master Rodne studije, Univerzitet u Beogradu, Fakultet političkih nauka, Beograd, Srbija

VLADISLAV ŠĆEPANOVIĆ

COMMISSIONER
KOMESAR

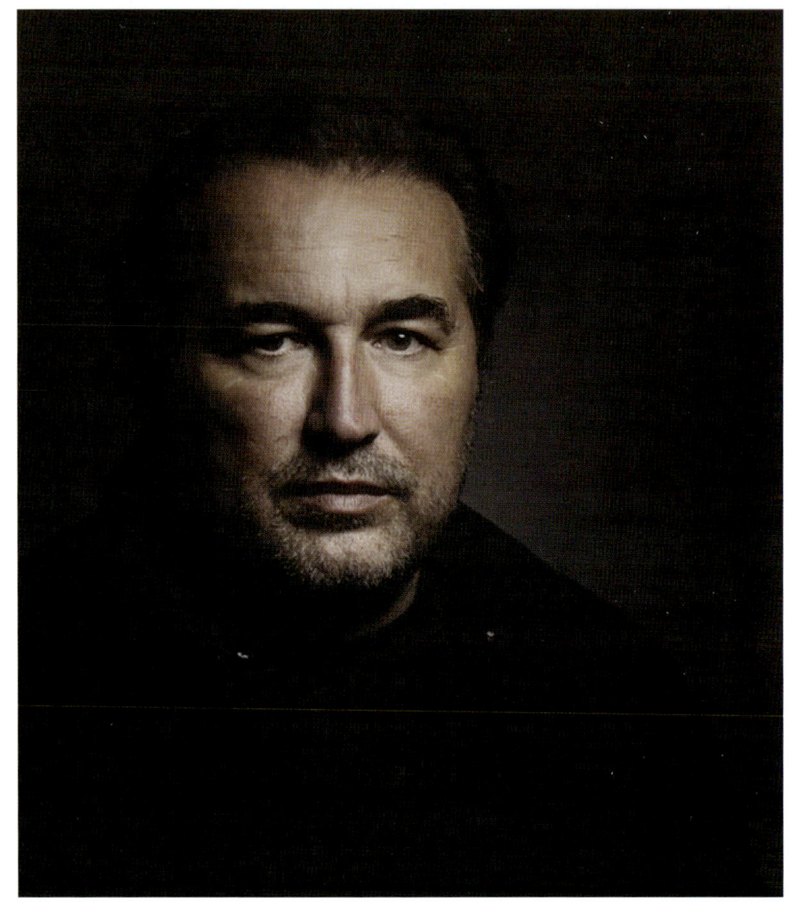

Photography / Fotografija
Nebojša Babić

BIOGRAPHY

Vladislav Šćepanović, born in 1971 in Nikšić, Montenegro, graduated from the University of Montenegro Faculty of Fine Arts in Cetinje in 1994. He earned his master's degree from the University of Arts in Belgrade, Faculty of Applied Arts, in 1996. In 2009, he attained his doctorate in the field of theory of arts and media from the Interdisciplinary Studies department at the University of Arts in Belgrade, under the guidance of Dr. Divna Vuksanović.

From 2013 to 2014, Šćepanović served as Acting Director at the Museum of Contemporary Art, Belgrade, followed by his tenure as President of the Board of Directors from 2019 to 2021. Presently, he holds the position of Director at the Museum of Contemporary Art of Montenegro, alongside his role as a full-time professor at the Faculty of Applied Arts, University of Arts in Belgrade.

His artistic pursuits have spanned the globe, with over thirty solo exhibitions and participation in numerous group exhibitions in cities including Banja Luka, Belgrade, Budva, Grožnjan, Hoboken, Houston, New York, Novi Sad, Osijek, Paris, Podgorica, Pohang, Tokyo, Venice and Washington.

Additionally, he has authored a monograph and several theoretical texts on art and media theory.

BIOGRAFIJA

Vladislav Šćepanović (1971) je rođen u Nikšiću. Diplomirao je na Fakultetu likovnih umjetnosti na Cetinju 1994. godine, a magistrirao je na Fakultetu primenjenih umetnosti u Beogradu 1996. godine. Doktorirao je na polju teorije umjetnosti i medija na Interdisciplinarnim doktorskim studijama, Univerziteta umetnosti u Beogradu 2009. godine, pod mentorstvom profesorke dr Divne Vuksanović.

Redovni je profesor na Fakultetu primjenjenih umjetnosti u Beogradu. Funkciju predsjednika Upravnog odbora Muzeja savremene umetnosti u Beogradu obavljao je od 2019. do 2021. godine, dok je u istoj ustanovi funkciju vršioca dužnosti obavljao periodu 2013/2014. godine. Direktor je Muzeja savremene umjetnosti Crne Gore.

Izlagao je na preko 30 samostalnih i više grupnih izložbi u Parizu, Tokiju, Njujorku, Venecij, Hjustonu, Hobokenu, Vašingtonu, Pohangu (Koreja), Podgorici, Budvi, Beogradu, Osijeku, Novom Sadu, Grožnjanu, Banja Luci...

Objavio je jednu monografiju i više naučnih tekstova iz oblasti Teorija umjetnosti i medija.

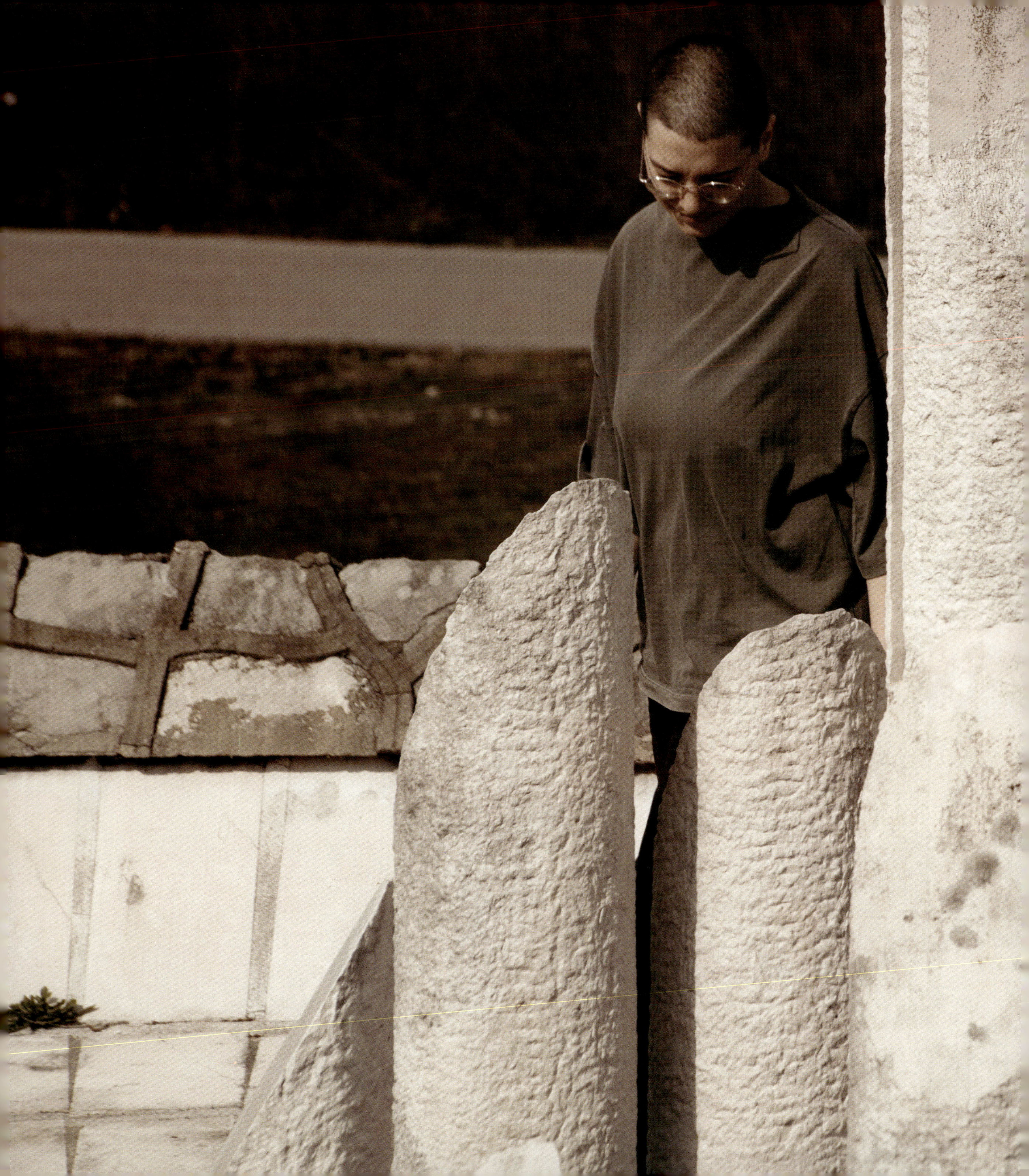

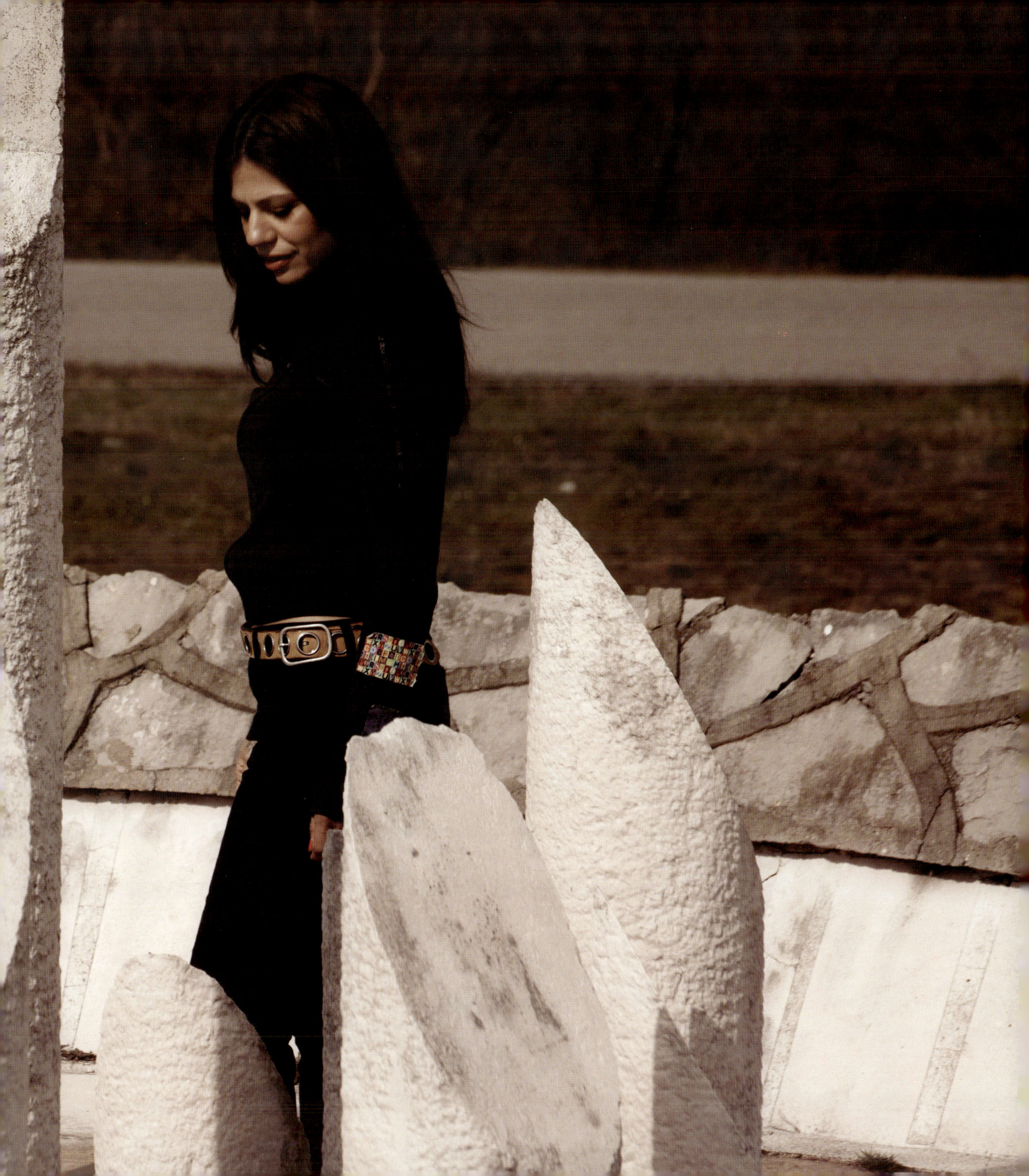

IMPRINT / IMPRESUM

Darja Bajagić
It Takes an Island to Feel This Good
Pavilion of Montenegro
60th International Art Exhibition –
La Biennale di Venezia
20.04 – 24.11.2024.

This catalog is published on the occasion of the exhibition Darja Bajagić — *It Takes an Island to Feel This Good,* commissioned by Vladislav Šćepanović and curated by Ana Simona Zelenović, for the Pavilion of Montenegro at the 60th International Art Exhibition – La Biennale di Venezia, Biennale Arte 2024, in Venice, Italy. / Ovaj katalog je objavljen povodom izložbe Darja Bajagić — *It Takes an Island to Feel This Good,* čiji je komesar Vladislav Šćepanović, a kustoskinja Ana Simona Zelenović, za Crnogorski paviljon na 60. Međunarodnoj izložbi umjetnosti – La Biennale di Venezia, u Veneciji, Italija.

EXHIBITION / IZLOŽBA

Commissioner / Komesar
Vladislav Šćepanović

Curator / Kustoskinja
Ana Simona Zelenović

Architects / Arhitekti
Predrag Krstić, Andrea Pajković

Assistant to the Commissioner / Asistentkinja komesara
Danica Bogojević

Technical Team / Tehnička ekipa
Prele Prelević, Nemanja Radević, Rajko Raičević, Novica Vuković

CATALOG / KATALOG

Editors / Urednice
Darja Bajagić, Ana Simona Zelenović

Texts / Tekstovi
Ingrid Luquet-Gad, Ana Simona Zelenović

Translation / Prevod
Darja Bajagić (EN)
Marko Mladenović (ME)

Proofreading / Lektura
Darja Bajagić (EN)
Jesi Khadivi (EN)
Tijana Rakočević (ME)

Layout Design / Dizajn preloma
Anđela Čpajak

Cover Design / Dizajn korice
Darja Bajagić

Photography of the Artwork / Fotografije umjetničkog djela
Marijana Janković

Photography of the Artist and curator / Fotografije umjetnice i kustoskinje
Geray Mena

Printing / Štampa
DPC Podgorica,
Podgorica, Montenegro

Print Run / Tiraž
600

Image Credits / Zasluge za slike
© Darja Bajagić
Geray Mena,
pp. 03, 93, 95, 104, 107, 116, 117
Marijana Janković,
pp. 43, 44, 45, 46, 47, 48, 49, 50 ,51, 53, 54, 55, 56, 57, 58, 59, 61, 62, 63, 54, 65, 66, 67, 68, 69, 71, 72, 73, 74, 75, 76, 77, 78, 79, 81, 82, 83, 84, 85, 86, 87, 88, 89

ORGANIZATION / ORGANIZACIJA

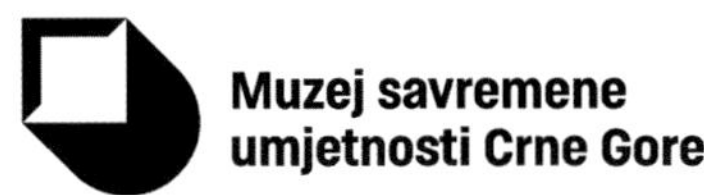

Museum of Contemporary Art of Montenegro / Muzej savremene umjetnosti Crne Gore

SPONSOR / POKROVITELJ

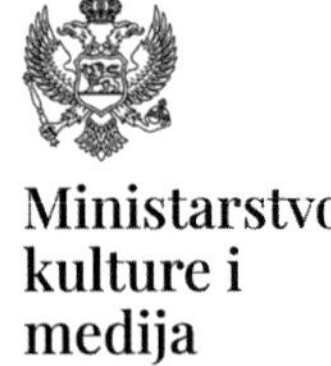

Ministry of Culture and Media of Montenegro / Ministarstvo kulture i medija Crne Gore

Published and distributed by
Mousse Publishing
Contrappunto s.r.l.
via Pier Candido Decembrio 28,
20137, Milan–Italy

Available through:
Mousse Publishing, Milan
moussemagazine.it

First edition: 2024

Printed in Montenegro by
DPC Podgorica

ISBN 978-88-6749-633-4

€ 27 / $ 30

© 2024 Museum of Contemporary Art of Montenegro, Mousse Publishing, Darja Bajagić (the artist), the authors of the texts

All works by Darja Bajagić: © 2024

All rights reserved. No part of this publication may be reproduced in any form or by any electronic means without prior written permission from the copyright holders.

The publisher would like to thank all those who have kindly given their permission for the reproduction of material for this book. Every effort has been made to obtain permission to reproduce the images and texts in this book. However, as is standard editorial policy, the publisher is at the disposal of copyright holders and undertakes to correct any omissions or errors in future editions.